OVERCOMING SPIRITUAL DRYNESS

By

IDONGEST OKPOMBOR

Overcoming Spiritual Dryness

Published by:

Kings View Publishing House

Tbilisi, Georgia.

www.kingsviewbooks.com

E-mail: enquiries@kingsviewbooks.com

+234-703-535-8454; +995-568-286-737

For information, please address:

IDONGESIT OKPOMBOR

E-mail: id_degt@yahoo.com

+995-568-286-737

Unless otherwise stated, all Scripture quotations are taken from the King James Version of the Holy Bible.

Contents

DEDICATION

I dedicate this great work of grace first, to my beloved sister according to the Gospel, **PASTOR FRANCA BOCO,** whose sincere love for me and the outworking of God in me' almost cost her life..."

I also dedicate this wonderful work of mercy, to the wounded Christian soldier, who finds it so difficult to, but greatly longs to get right back up again.

And to the child of God who hungers and thirsts for Him, so much that he daily cries from deep within, "My soul thirsteth for God, for the living God: when shall I come and appear before God?"

Finally, I dedicate this great book, to the Body of Christ in these last days, and the Minister who longs to stay close to his Master's heart.

ACKNOWLEDGEMENTS

Thanks to God for making me a blessing to countless many. My Daddy and Mummy (Mr. & Mrs. E.U. Okpombor), "your flair for writing and love for education have made the man of me...your blood flows through my veins.

Thanks to Evang. (Mrs. Helen Ukpabio for finding time to go through this book and write the foreword. Thanks also to Rev. (Engr.) Ndukwe Roberts and Rev. (Dr.) Demas Abraham for their useful suggestions and encouraging comments after going through the manuscript.

Mrs. Pat Emesih proof-read the very first manuscript and has ever since continued to find out if it has been published. Dr. Elijah Ukpabio did a lot of restructuring in the earliest presentation of the work. My aunties and sisters according to the Gospel – Patience Uquak, Rosaline Itam, Charity Onyegbule, and Elizabeth Ukpuho – did the final proof-reading. They all put me on the pathway towards prolific writing. I'm grateful.

To the members of the Liberty Gospel Church Youth choir from which originated this book, I express my sincere love and gratitude. My friends: Simon Sunday, Akwaowo Joshua, Jesse Elijah, Linda Itang, Christiana Olory, to mention but a few, have been such a great encouragement to me.

To Ennie (Arit Effiong), who exercised so much patience in typesetting this book, and to elder and Mrs. Itang who allowed me the use of their computer system to effect most of the corrections, I say thank you.

Finally, to everyone who contributed in one way or the other to make this work a success, I'm grateful.

FOREWORD

Having read through the book, "Overcoming Spiritual Dryness", I find it to be a must-read by every born again Christian, whose appetite for God and spiritual hunger has greatly declined. I do not intend to only refer those who are on the verge of collapse, but also, whoever thinks he is standing in the Faith.

There is a lot to be bothered about, and a lot to be discouraged from, but there are rare means and devices to bring back or restore a battered, confused, discouraged, and non-existing appetite for God. The reason is, they all have been going to church and hearing the Gospel, before becoming so empty and dry, that spiritually they are ALMOST dead.

This book explains the state of the true Church of Christ in these last days. You have more backsliders in Church than the believers; more hypocrites than the true worshippers; and more of peripheral Christians than righteous believers in the church.

This book will help restore a sinking Church and a collapsing Minister whose joy for service is gone. He has been struggling daily to live right, without taking time to deliberate or prepare himself for the benefit of the flock.

When personal needs and demands overtake the Ministerial mind; when Christians measure success by worldly standards; when decisions for spiritual things are looked at, judged, and considered by sight and not by faith; then of truth, a state of DRYNESS has set in.   When God is only given a second and not a first place, then, one must accept the truth and quickly seek restoration and refreshing.

The Word of God is still a very strong and powerful factor to restore an insensitive heart to God.   Read this book! It is the best pill for a spiritually declines state.   This book must never stop with you only...get others to get it and read.

LADY APOSTLE HELEN UKPABIO

Calabar, Nigeria

PREFACE

Mary had to break the alabaster box, for its fragrance to reach others. Jesus had to break the fish with which He fed the five thousand before He gave it. God delights in using 'broken things' I have come to deeply understand.

At many times in different years, God led me through several experiences, to help me understand what it meant for others to pass through what He intended that I write about. Severally, I have been broken, mended, and moulded again, just to be made a blessing to others, and I am grateful that finally, I am. I have realized that, to be where I am, I needed every bit of where I found myself. Most gladly, therefore, like the Apostle Paul, "I glory in my infirmities, that the power of Christ may radiate through me."

God knows much better than I can express what this book will do in your life, as you prayerfully read it. This only, I can humbly say: this book will make you want to put it down and think or pray for yourself...and if it does, please do.

Idongesit Okpombor

Tbilisi, Georgia.

INTRODUCTION

One fateful day, I went through my little photo album. It was not the first time I had gone through it that way. Something seemed to strike my heart each time I looked past a particular photograph.

The striking feeling seemed to intensify in my heart with deep sorrow within as I tried to take a more careful look at that photograph. Something out of the ordinary was happening to me, and I needed to understand what it was.

This particular photograph was taken some two years back with three other friends after a wonderful youth week programme, which we had each yielded ourselves fully to be used of the Holy Spirit.

I had spoken on that wonderful Friday night and also given such a soft but heart pricking special number on the Sunday morning of that programme. I felt heaven in the church. I felt like I was carrying God around. It was such an amazing experience.

This photograph taken at the end of the programme seemed to have been more than just an image of the outward, but also a reflection of what I had been carrying within.

As I closely looked at it with an intensifying godly sorrow in my heart, I seemed to hear the 'me' in the photograph telling the 'me' out here in a sorrowfully soft and gentle but clear tone, "You are no longer who you used to be."

Cold tears flowed deep down the vessels of my broken heart as I closed the album and spoke those heart pricking but true words to myself; "I am not longer who I used to be." I was in a state of spiritual degeneration and had better known that, if I was ever to recover.

I was ebbing spiritually in such a slow manner that I hardly could notice. I had pulled off that "ornament of a meek and quiet spirit, which is in the sight of God of great price" without any knowledge. I was spiritually dry.

Now, I have come to realize that many a time, God allows us to pass through certain things so that He might prune or cut us to size again. Spiritual dryness is dangerous and terrible too.

But God sometimes does allow us to pass through some of these things so that He might humble us, show how over self-confident, careless, and spiritually myopic we have become, or let us know that we are drifting away from our roots.

Sometimes, it allows us to be much more careful.

I do believe that some of the things we pass through are actually preparatory grounds for a higher level of service or relationship with God.

I do not, however, imply that God only uses bitter spiritual experiences, trials, and difficulties to lift us to higher heights, or lead us into a deeper relationship and closer walk with Him.

But when He does, "*we must*" as Watchman Nee once said, *realize that all the experiences, difficulties, and trials from the Lord are for our highest good.*"

I do think that most of the times God allows us to pass through Spiritual Dryness, He is simply telling us that the time is ripe for us to take another step unto a new and higher level of walk with Him.

I feel God does this because some of us get too quickly satisfied with the level we find ourselves in our relationship with Him, with so little or no desire for something greater.

I quite agree with Dr. Wesley Duewel that, "*We are too easily satisfied and glory in occasional past moments when God touched us by His power. We have become too complacent and too easily satisfied with* minimum *manifestations of His power."* And this 'complacency' A. W. Tozer says, *"Is a deadly foe of all spiritual growth."*

It is not God's will that we dwell for so long on a particular level of spiritual experience or relationship with Him, but rather, that we grow and experience higher heights and grounds as there is always a higher ground.

It was Dennis Kinlaw who very assuredly said, *"He does not want me to be the same next week that I was last week."* This is the simple truth!

Nevertheless, when we heartily return to the Lord after a bitter experience of spiritual dryness, He does not put us again on the former level we were. He does not take us back to where we were before that painful experience;

rather, He takes us to a new level entirely.

We do not relate with Him anymore in prayer the same way that we knew to do but deeper and much more loving than we ever could do. We develop a deeper longing for the Word, deeper than we have ever had.

Deeper revelations start flooding our inner man, and certain verses of Scripture we had once known become almost entirely new because of the depth of revelations we become exposed to.

In fact, everything about our relationship with Him assumes a new dimension.

He clothes us with a new glory. He does not give again the former glory, but a new glory – a latter glory. And

He had already promised us that the latter glory shall be greater than the former.

The latter glory of this house shall be greater than the former, says the Lord of hosts; - Haggai 2:9a (Berkeley)

The current state you find yourself in, is where this book is set to take you from, and God's awesome glory is what it is set to re-establish over your life, calling, purpose, and destiny.

See you on the GLORY side!

The Nature of Spiritual Dryness

"How tragic when a Christian leader, like Samson, has once known special times of the Lord's enabling when the spirit came upon him "in power" and then begins to rely on his own 'know how,' his busy endeavours, and his administrative skills more than on the Lord,"

Dr. Wesley Duewel

Chapter 1

What is Spiritual Dryness?

I feel it is easier to explain spiritual dryness as a state than define it as a term. When we look at it as a spiritual state, which we, at one time either get into or pass through, it becomes easier for us to understand its nature. The question, "What is the nature of spiritual dryness?" then becomes of greater benefit to us.

Spiritual Degeneration

Thus saith the LORD, What iniquity have your fathers found in me, that they are gone far from me, and have walked after vanity, and are become vain? **Jeremiah 2:5**

Spiritual dryness is a state of spiritual degeneration. The spiritually dry Christian realizes that he is no longer the same person he must have known himself to be some days, weeks, months, or years past.

Actually, he should not remain the same person he was yesterday, as long as spiritual life experiences and growth processes are concerned. He has to grow. And if he really does, his today must always be better than yesterday. Else, remaining as much the same today as he was yesterday would be nothing else but spiritual stagnation.

However, in spiritual dryness, he realizes that he does not even measure up with his spiritual standing of yesterday. He may still be doing the same things(s) he used to do: preaching, singing, teaching, etc., but he simply cannot measure up with who he was yesterday. He has degenerated spiritually.

He then notices that his initial spiritual carefulness ebbs daily into unnoticed carelessness. And soon he becomes like "everybody" or "anybody" else in words, deeds, and actions.

Being like anybody or everybody else is such a dangerous affair because, there are things that God would not want us to do as close children of His, not exactly because they are sinful, but because of our level of consecration to Him.

There are things He would not be happy if we touched, though every other Christian might be touching.

There are places other Christians may comfortably go to, which He may not want us to go.

There are also, things He would not be pleased to see us do or hear us say, which others may be saying or doing without the least compunction.

He delights in separating us to Himself.

In Numbers chapter 12:6-8 we see a practical example of this:

And he said, Hear now my words: If there be a prophet among you, I the LORD will make myself known unto him in a vision, and will speak unto him in a dream. My servant Moses is not so, who is faithful in all mine house. With him will I speak mouth to mouth, even apparently, and not in dark speeches; and the similitude of the

LORD shall he behold... **Numbers 12:6-8** P a g e

To the children of Israel, the Scripture declares that God *revealed* His acts, but to Moses *He revealed His ways* (Psalms 103:7).

Moses *was* a different person in God's sight because he had a different level of consecration. And God brings the same realization to every child of His, who seeks to get closer to Him.

That is why we realize that, as we grow in Him, as our thirst for more of Him increases, as our earnest desire to know Him intensifies, many things that were once important to us become very unimportant.

The spiritually dry Christian loses sight of this consecration, and soon becomes like everyone else in his day-to-day living and dealing. He then tends to progress in a direction in which sacred things gradually get treated as secular things without giving the least consideration to the Divine consequences that should likely follow.

"A man goes downward once he looks down on his consecration."

Chapter 2

Evidence of Self-ability

The true Christian finds neither the least comfort nor pleasure in doing anything within or without, except with the grace and Divine backing from above. He honours, treasures, and esteems the backing from above more than the task below.

Thus, he will rather be much with God than with men, and will rather be useful to God than be famous among men. He, therefore, treasures above all things, his private or personal communion with His Master. To him, a day does not begin until he has satisfactorily spoken with His Saviour and Lord.

When he speaks in public prayer, he speaks with such deep conviction as with He whom he consistently speaks. He is no much better at expressing himself outside his closet than he does inside.

Who he is and what he does in the place where men can see, is no more than a replica of who he is and what he does in the place where men cannot see.

The spiritually dry Christian, on the other hand, gives unnoticingly, more room to the ephemeral and trivial and gradually loses the true grace and spiritual backing that propels the spirit.

He finds it unfearfully easy to begin a day without the Lord, and perhaps equally end it without Him. That does not prevent him anyway, from acting as a public prayer warrior, while he goes back to continue a private prayer mediocre.

And if a minister or preacher, with a whisper of few minutes to the Lord, he seems able to minister in public more than he could, when he spent longer times with his Master.

'After all,' he feels, *'a time comes when one is so close to God that he must not spend as much time with Him before ministering!'*

He soon becomes much with men and less with God, and the more hold he has on that which men can see or hear and be elated, the less grip he lays on that which God alone can give.

Now friend, do you not see that things are changing?

Can you not notice your inclination to the physical and declination from the spiritual?

Have you not noticed that you are the same member of the congregation as of old but not the same contributor to that congregation spiritually?

Do you not notice that the choir remains the same yet you are not the same music minister that once led a whole congregation some years past into an uncontrollable flood of tears?

Can you not recognize that the pulpit remains the same, and the duty the same but you, the Pastor, are changing?

Have not the revelational power of God's Word that sent men down the aisles to the altar weeping with tears of true repentance not been replaced with talent, oratory, and eloquence?

"How tragic when a Christian leader, like Samson, has once known special times of the Lord's enabling when the spirit came upon him "in power" and then begins to rely on his own 'know how,' his busy endeavours, and his administrative skills more than on the Lord," Dr. Wesley Duewel wrote.

Oh friend, do you not see that more of your power is becoming evident and less of God's?

Is more of your ability and strength not becoming evident and less of His?

Have you not now made so literal the words, *"By strength shall no man prevail,"* and *His strength is made perfect in my weakness"*, which were as a motto to you in the days wherewith your weaknesses were so evident both before you and the men around you?

Do you not realize that the song, "*I have no of else but thee,*" and the word, "*that I may know Him,*" are dying out of your heart?

Dr. R.T. Kendall related an experience that I'll love to share:

"A minister friend of mine was trying to win a prominent lawyer to his church, and finally, the man agreed to come and hear him preach. So my friend worked doubly hard on his sermon, and after the service was over, thought, 'I've really done it!', and he couldn't wait to get the lawyer's reaction.

"The man said, 'I've got a book in my office with every word of your sermon in it. Come around

tomorrow morning and I'll show it to you.'

"Well, my friend hardly slept that night. Nine O'clock the next morning found him as the office. The lawyer handed him a dictionary and said, 'Words, preacher – just words.'

You see, how *much* of the Lord, His power, and anointing we have, and experience depends on how *less* of us we have, for He can only increase where we decrease.

Chapter 3

Degeneration of Spiritual Fruit

But the fruit of the Spirit is love, joy, peace, longsuffering, gentleness, goodness, faith, Meekness, temperance.... **Galatians 5:22-23**

Spiritual dryness is a state in which the fruit of the Spirit degenerates while the works of the flesh gradually become evident.

The spiritually dry Christian, who had once manifested the fruit of the Spirit, soon experiences the contrary. He finds it relatively easier to condemn than commend. And there is the possibility of losing that gentle spirit which accommodates and endures men.

He soon realizes that he seems to be fed up with everything, but somehow cannot stop attending church.

When he finds himself in church, everything seems to be going wrong. It is as if the announcements are too many, the choir looks too dull, and the message is too long.

He just cannot stand when others are standing to pray. Those who pray 'too much' seem to be 'over-spiritual,' and those who worship the Lord beside him and in the process burst into tears seem to be 'showing off 'or disturbing his peace.

He realizes that in a short while he becomes a professor of skepticism and criticism:

"Oh, the choristers sang off-key... The pastor dressed like colonial police.. There were too many offerings taken..."

"Well, if at any time in our Christian lives we fail to manifest the fruit of the Holy Spirit, we may likely manifest the fruit of an unholy spirit."

Chapter 4

Exaggeration of Fleshly Needs

For the flesh lusteth against the Spirit, and the Spirit against the flesh: and these are contrary the one to the other: so that ye cannot do the things that ye would. **Galatians 5:17**

Spiritual dryness is a state in which the desire and need of the body become more exaggerated and overwhelm the desire of the spirit.

All of a sudden, one starts imagining that he has not been having enough rest, and begins to develop a greater desire to sleep than to pray.

He no longer observes midnight prayers, and no more one, two, or even three hours of quiet time; ten minutes is enough.

Preference is given to a little stroll over attending a Bible study or to a doss down on an early Sunday morning over attending a Sunday school class.

His watchmen are blind: they are all ignorant, they are all dumb dogs, they cannot bark; sleeping, lying down, loving to slumber. **Isaiah 56:10**

If fasting is ever observed, such a fast must ends when the breakfast is ready. Having a personal fast soon becomes one of the most difficult heights to attain.

It seems as though one always hears a voice that constantly says, "You are emaciating. If you dare fast again, you will become bonier than a crucified Jesus or a resurrecting Lazarus."

For many walk, of whom I have told you often......Whose end is destruction, whose God is their belly.... **Philipians 3:18**

The belly then becomes one of the greatest idols with which to battle. Such a one would likely take a fast only when there is a compulsory one in the church.

Where it becomes 'too much' – say two or three times in one month – an objection is secretly raised: "Brethren, let us not be so heavenly conscious that we become earthly useless!"

There is a greatly waning desire for the things of the spirit and a proportionate increase in the desire for bodily satisfaction.

"The greatest victory a man can have in his lifetime is the victory over self."

Chapter 5

Death of Conscience

Spiritual dryness describes a period in a life in which the fear of God and the witness of the spirit cease to be.

The spiritually fresh Christian takes every action according to the Word of God. He desires above all else to please God in everything – *"Proving what is acceptable unto the Lord"*.

Each time something wrong is done, there is the feeling that God is hurt. This is proof of the aliveness of his conscience to the witness of God's Spirit.

Now take, for instance, someone spoke to you in the wrong manner and probably hurt you. You would love to respond, but considering what you were about to say, the fear of God would not allow you say it.

Or, let's say you found yourself in a situation where you would have almost laughed down a person to public embarrassment but there was a witness of the spirit: *"Don't do it, lest you hurt him."*

Consider also that you witnessed your minister make a mistake on the pulpit, but just as you were about joining a 'crew' of church critics to talk about it, something ministered to you: *"Why don't you pray for him?"*

These were each, the witness of the spirit.

In spiritual dryness, the witness of the spirit is deadly silent.

One who is spiritually dry seems to be at peace to say or do anything without any fear of God. Such a person finds it easier to give reasons for his actions than accept the simplest correction.

His conscience bears him no witness any longer. So, he sins and finds that it just looks ordinary. The things he once controlled then begin to control and rule over him.

He really may still be preaching, teaching, leading a Sunday school, or choir, but while he gives to others a promise of liberty, he remains a slave of corruption.

During spiritual freshness, a Christian who misses his quiet time does not seem to feel okay throughout the day. It is just as if something is missing, or something is going wrong somewhere.

But, the spiritually dry Christian can stay for days without having his quiet time, and yet everything looks normal. Prayer or no prayer, Bible study or no Bible study, he is comfortable. After all, he is still regular in church activities.

Brother Gbile Akanni is right on target when he writes that, *"When a man loses his spiritual sensitivity, many things will be lost from his life before he knows it."*

"A believer with a deadly silent spiritual conscience is equivalent to a sleeping soldier in a battlefield."

Chapter 6

A State of Spiritual Indecision

Spiritual dryness is a pitiful state in which the believer neither finds himself in the world nor fully in the Lord.

He does not decline completely into the world, lest people say he has backslidden: He still keeps to the doctrines of his church, and would not abandon his responsibility, but within him is a serious struggle going on between two great opposing parties.

He is in a state of spiritual indecision, which is no more than an application for admission into the school of hypocrisy.

He is neither alive nor dead, neither on the mountain nor in the valley, neither on fire nor in water, and neither hot nor cold – he is lukewarm.

I know thy works, that thou art neither cold nor hot: I would thou wert cold or hot.16 So then because thou art lukewarm, and neither cold nor hot, I will spue thee out of my mouth. **Revelation 3:15-16**

"To live yet neither fully in the Lord nor fully in the world is the greatest way a man can cheat himself."

Chapter 7

Loss of Vision

I will finally use an experience in Judges 16:19, 21, to describe spiritual dryness.

And she made him sleep upon her knees; and she called for a man, and she caused him to shave off the seven locks of his head; and she began to afflict him, **_and his strength went from him._** *But the Philistines took him,* **_and put out his eyes_***, and brought him down to Gaza, and bound him with fetters of brass;* **_and he did grind in the prison house_***.* **Judges 16:19, 21**

Let us carefully note the underlined statement, each of which portrays a state of dryness in a believer.

And His Strength Went From Him

Spiritual dryness is a state of loss of strength and power.

But they that wait upon the LORD shall renew their strength..... **Isaiah 40:31**

There is slack in strength because there has been no waiting upon the Lord anymore.

What strength?

Strength to run the race. Strength to serve the Lord and save the lost. And Strength to impart life to others.

Once the strength is lost, serving the Lord becomes a burden. Saving the lost becomes boring and tiring. And imparting life to others – whether through daily contact or from the pulpit – becomes the most hypocritical lifestyle to combat with, for only life can beget life!

Accompanying the loss of strength is the loss of power: Power over the will, power over sin, and power to walk right, talk right, and live right.

"Loss of strength is the magnifying glass through which backsliding is seen as a beautiful venture."

And Put Out His Eyes

In spiritual dryness, there is a loss of vision, just like Samson lost his eyes.

There is a loss of Calvary's touch.

The visions of rapture, of heaven, and the judgment seat are lost. The spiritually dry Christian does not have such alertness about them anymore.

Hence, his thoughts and actions can no more be guided in that direction.

The visions of rapture, of heaven, and the judgment seat, have real power to control a believer's thoughts and actions to a great extent.

His character and life change when he loses this wonderful vision(s).

He would then walk, talk, live and act as though there were no more heaven, judgment, and marriage supper of the Lamb's bride.

Samson had lost his eyes and would therefore no longer be able to fulfill the purpose God Has sent him to his people.

When spiritual dryness sets in, one seems to lose the vision he once had.

Take, for instance, you have the vision to teach men, women, and maybe youths into the kingdom of God through the Sunday school.

This was what caused you to groan in the spirit in half nights and whole nights of prayer.

This vision will not allow you to teach your Sunday school class without first holding onto the horns of the altar for hours before.

You may not have known what others were, but you knew who you were. Until the impact of the Word was prayed into existence and the hearts of men were made soft as the grass of the field, you could not stand to teach.

Now you have lost that vision. You can now get up from slumber at any time and teach your class. Sometimes, you can even revise your Sunday school lesson on your way to the church on Sunday morning, without any feeling for the souls that you intend to teach.

You have lost your vision like Samson. You have lost your consecration. You have forgotten the purpose of your call. You are, therefore, living without a goal, focus, or sense of direction.

"Living, working and acting without a goal, focus, or sense of direction is like earnestly playing football without a goalpost." – Elijah Ukpabio

Can you still remember those days you had a longing to join the choir? Do you still remember the vision that dangled within your spirit night and day as you kept thinking about the impact of the music ministry upon the lives of men?

Can you, like me, still remember that fateful night when you fell on your face and cried, *"Jesus, you are the praise that I need. You are the applause my spirit seeks. Not the praise of men, nor the applause of the world. But all I need, all I seek, even above life, is that you make me a man after your heart. Use me as a vessel unto honour. Flow through me and reach out to men..."*

Do you remember the tears that wetted the floor that night as you prayed and groaned before God that as you minister in songs the next day, He would give unto His people, *the oil of joy for mourning, and the garment of praise for the spirit of heaviness?*.

If you can recall very well, your vision was to see men saved, healed, delivered, restored, and touched in a different dimension by God, as you ministered in songs. That vision had control of your life. You could not talk to everybody or anybody because you were carrying something.

Every other person could just sing but you would not get to the stage to minister until you had been wetted with the dew from above.

All these were because you had a vision burning within your spirit for fulfillment.

Now, things are different. You have lost that vision. That is why you can wake up and sing like every other person.

You have lost that vision. That is why you can joke with the delicate parts of Delilah's body without sensing the danger ahead.

Oh, friend, you have lost that vision! That is why the technicalities of your ministrations are nowadays more important to you than the spiritual impact of it upon lives.

Carnal comparison with others, of your abilities, has taken the place of utter helplessness and inability which you once confessed before the Lord in time past.

Let me ask you: How did you feel, the very first time you were given an opportunity to preach or teach the Word of God before a small or large congregation?

If you do not remember how you felt, I can help remind you. If it was a small congregation or house fellowship group, you felt like pouring out all that was within you.

On the other hand, if it was a large church congregation, your excitement was mixed with fear and fright.

You fell on your face before God and expressed how helpless you were. You told Him, if He does not speak, no other word will be able to produce such a strong conviction upon the longing hearts of men as His.

In both cases, you had a vision. Your vision was to see God flow through you to affect the lives of helpless men and women.

But look at your attitude in teaching that house fellowship today. Have you not become so used to the responsibility?

Look at your attitude as you pastor that large congregation today. Have you not lost the vision that kept you on course?

"A vision lost is a mission unaccomplished. An unaccomplished mission is as good as a stillbirth."

And He Did Grind in the Prison House

Samson began to grind in the prison house.

His muscles were growing fatter, but he had lost his hair – his glory and strength.

When spiritually dry, one may really preach better, but with stale oil.

One may sing better than he may, but the secret place constantly accuses.

One may gain fame and recognition for a good display of gifts, talents, and head knowledge, but has lost something greater than them.

I agree with Brother Gbile Akanni that, *"There is a tendency to equate powerful preaching with powerful living. But this is the deception that destroys men of God. Pulpit anointing that is not commensurate with personal anointing is a deception that will destroy any man of God."*

Such a man is no more than a 'grinder in a prison house,' with fatter muscles and less hair – greater demonstrations with less glory.

Friend, do you not see that you have lost the glory cloud – the source of your strength?

"It is better to live a warrior and be known by none than live in secret defeats yet be known a warrior by all."

CAUSES OF SPIRITUAL DRYNESS

Why is Your Spiritual Life Recently Becoming Such an Uphill Task?

Give it a thought:

✓ Why do you wake up with *little or no desire to read the Bible or pray?*

✓ Why do you feel *so little energy for spiritual things* but still bubble with so much energy for other life activities?

✓ Why are you getting *tired of fellowship with the brethren?*

✓ Why are you experiencing *a diminution in your love and desire for God and His presence?*

This part explains all the Bible says about spiritual dryness and indirectly gives the keys to spiritual growth.

Chapter 8

What Causes Spiritual dryness?

...And, let everyone that nameth the name of Christ depart from iniquity.

2 Timothy 2:19

The root cause of spiritual dryness is sin - whether it is that of omission or of commission, inward or outward. Sin in all its ramifications is exceedingly sinful and must be seen as such. For, nothing else better commissions and conditions a man for a thorough and painful fall like sin.

"Ah! Give me, Lord, the tender heart that trembles at the approach of sin; a godly fear of sin impart, implant and

root it deep within, that I may dread thy gracious power, and never dare offend thee more." – Charles Wesley

Sins of Omission and Commission

There are sins of omission and there are also sins of commission. We get into a sin of omission when we *omit to do what God has asked us to do.* For instance, the Bible urges us to pray. The Bible says in Matthew 6:7, *"But when you pray"* and not *"if you pray"*. *"If"* makes it optional, but 'when' indicates a compulsory task. When we neglect praying, therefore, we voluntarily get into a sin of omission.

Refusing to go and win souls is also a sin of omission.

For though I preach the gospel, I have nothing to glory of: for necessity is laid upon me. **1Corinthians 9:16b**

And all things are of God, who hath reconciled us to Himself by Jesus Christ and hath given unto us the ministry of reconciliation. - **2 Corinthians 5:18-19**

Neglect of evangelism is, therefore, a sin of omission.

Pastor William Kumuyi once wrote, *"Do you know that eighty-five souls die every minute? Unfortunately, they die without anyone showing them the way to eternal life. They die without hope. They die and go to hell. They die without the forgiveness of their sins because you have not told them about salvation."*

And with such a deep burden, therefore, the Apostle Paul would write, *Yea, woe is unto me, if I preach not the gospel!* 1 Corinthians 9:16

"A man without passion for perishing souls is a man that may well lack compassion for a dying one, and a man without compassion for another is the devil's sweetheart."

Equally, not too long after we become Christians, we get introduced to the inner speaking voice of the Triune God in our inward being. Then the closer we get, the more deeply we learn of Him and the more ashamed we gradually become of most of our early past actions.

However, as we get closer and closer with a deeper and higher consecration, we realize that this inner voice begins to speak to us of many things which we have either relegated to the background, forgotten, or taken for granted.

It may be a reminder of some little debts unpaid or restitution yet not made. That may be the restitution of a little Christian literature or tape we got from a friend to read or listen to, which has suddenly become part of our own personal shelf.

It may also be an unbroken wrong relationship with the same or opposite sex, which has become a canker-worm to our walk with Him.

It may equally be an apology He demands we make, which we may have been fighting against for years.

It may yet be a reminder of a pledge or promise we made but left unfulfilled.

However, the basic truth is this: the closer we get and the higher our consecration, the more we hear from Him in those quiet moments with Him, deep things of which some may actually be against our individual wills.

In any case, whether in line with or against our wills, it is sinful to omit from putting right, a wrong which the Divine inner speaking voice points to us. In many cases, they may not be wrong from our individual views, perspectives, and judgments. But if God says they are, they simply are wrong.

Whenever the Lord brings to the light of our remembrance, a debt unpaid, restitution unmade, pledge or promise unfulfilled, a wrong relationship unbroken, etc., He simply implies that we comply. It is a sin of omission when we either neglect or show a lack of concern towards such inner promptings. The consequence – some of which may actually be eternal – may always be far-reaching.

Therefore to him that knoweth to do good, and doeth it not, to him it is sin. **James 4:17-5:1**

On the other hand, we get into a sin of commission when we either consciously or unconsciously do what God has asked us not to do. For instance, if you steal or tell a lie, you *commit* sin. Whether you lie with a man or woman physically who is not your husband or wife, you get into a sin of commission.

"Sin is exceedingly sinful."

Outward and Inward Sins

There are inward sins as well as outward sins. Let us assume as Christians we steal, fight, kill, or do any of the outward wrongs, which others can see, we commit a sin outwardly.

But there are times when things happen and we show no immediate reaction, and sometimes none thereafter; yet deep within us, we boil and fume, and nobody can see, except God. Those inward fits of anger, bitterness, hatred, worry, lust, etc., which cannot be seen are all inward sins.

Think about it: There are times we speak as believers. The things we say may actually be true, but hidden behind our words is the spirit of criticism, condemnation, envy, jealousy, pride, or self-importance. These are inward sins.

"What is hidden behind things is what matter the most." – watchman Nee

Willful Sins

Willful sins, as the name implies, are sins we purposely and willingly get into. In other words, one may really know that what we are about to do is sinful but get on to do it nonetheless.

Such sins lead to spiritual dryness. Once the sin is committed, the soul gets surrounded with such a great cloud of guilt and regret that leaves us spiritually confused for days, weeks, and perhaps months.

The 'little' immoral filthiness a believer freely or consciously gets involved in today can turn him into a handkerchief in the hands of the devil tomorrow.

The boldness he once had in approaching the throne of grace will be replaced with fear. He is afraid if God will still hear him. And sometimes, the devil tells him that he is wasting his time, and that it is better he just backs out.

Such a believer most likely becomes so confused that he begins to live from day to day like an ordinary person and no longer as a soldier does.

The typical unbeliever operates in worldliness while the willful sinner operates in carnality. If care is not taken, there is the likelihood of falling back into the same sin.

Willfully getting into sin is such a dangerous affair: *for if we sin willfully after that we have received the knowledge of the truth, there remaineth no more sacrifice for sins.* – **Hebrews 10:26**

"*Show me a man that lacks control over his will and I'll show you a man always taken captive at will by the devil.*"

Presumptuous Sins

Presumptuous sins are sins that rule over or most often subdues a believer.

The believer may really hate getting into such sins but often finds himself helplessly in it.   He often does it against his personal will and ends up with regrets once it is over.

For I do not understand what I am doing. I do not do what I want to do but what I hate to do. – **Romans 7:15**

Sometimes, these sins were those which most often plagued and overpowered such a believer when he was yet unsaved. The devil, therefore, tempts him often, now that he is a believer, with the same things he was once used to.

If he was a hot-tempered person, the devil uses situations that provoke him to serious anger to tempt him.

If he had a strong sex drive as an unbeliever, Satan also uses things pertaining to that to tempt him now that he is a believer.

Most unbelievers develop serious habits they find difficult to break even after they become believers. These habits metamorphose, at most times, into presumptuous sins.

They find themselves getting into such sins even when they would not want to. At one time, they are faced with it, and just before they know it, they are at the altar confessing the same sin again.

For the good that I would I do not: but the evil which I would not, that I do. – **Romans 7:19**

Presumptuous sins are much more dangerous. They can keep a person longer in spiritual dryness because there is the tendency of being deceived into thinking that God will not forgive the sin anymore.

Such a person begins to feel that he has so disappointed God; that God will think He is being joked with, and may not even bend low to listen to him again. The result would always be such fear as drives him away from the presence of God.

He probably tends to see himself as being so unworthy, even to be in the presence of God, and soon develops the feeling that he is deceiving himself by continuing in God. This is a dangerous state!

Keep back thy servant also from **presumptuous sins**, *let them not have dominion over me.* – **Psalms 19:13**

Presumptuous or besetting sins lead directly into spiritual dryness, but many a time, it is actually the guilt that ensues that leads into this experience.

"The most painful defeat is that suffered when no one is around."

Spiritual Complacency and Carelessness

Spiritual Complacency can also cause spiritual dryness. This is a condition where a Christian feels satisfied for achieving some 'ground-breaking' landmarks in life and Ministry.

Success in Ministry relished for a prolonged time without further attempts of moving forward can eclipse a believer's spiritual dryness in such slow manners that they would unlikely notice.

"Spiritual carelessness is the 'regrets' history book of backslidden champions."

Chapter 9

Carelessness in Prayer

Prayer is the price of power. A prayerless Christian is a powerless Christian. Prayer is more than just talking to God, it is talking with God. To be much for God is to be much with God.

Spiritual dryness sets in when we become careless with our personal prayer lives. Backsliding you'll say, began when you committed sin, but I'd say no, your backsliding began when you became careless in prayer – when you stopped praying. "A praying man will stop sinning and a sinning man will stop praying," Leonard Ravenhill wrote.

Man is a tripartite being – made of spirit, soul, and body. Each of these: the spirit, soul, and body requires food to thrive well. Without natural food, the body cannot grow normally.

A man that eats good food regularly will grow healthier bodily than a man who either eats poorly or rarely eats.

Just as the body requires food for energy and normal growth, the spirit and the soul also need food to grow well. The food of the soul is the Word of God while the food of the spirit is prayer.

In essence, a Christian can no more grow spiritually without spiritual food than he can grow physically without physical food. Hence, the word, "pray without ceasing."

"Our number one weakness is not sin but prayerlessness" – Ernest Gruen

How Do We Become Careless In Prayer?

Knowledge of how we do need to pray will help us know about carelessness as it pertains to our prayer lives.

We should observe our fellowship with the Lord daily. *For which cause we faint not; but though our outward man perish;* **yet the inward man is renewed day by day.** - Corinthians 4:6

This renewal of the inward man – the spirit man – takes place only through daily prayer.

David cried unto God daily.

Be merciful unto me, O Lord; for I cry unto thee daily. – **Psalms 86:3**

Daniel prayed three times a day.

Brother Gbile Akanni wrote, *"If Daniel was a reputable prophet, I dare say it was his prayer life that released him into the prophetic office. His gifts and visions came forth very mightily because he fanned it to flame in the secret place of secret praying."*

Now when Daniel knew that the writing was signed, he went into his house; and his windows being open in his chamber toward Jerusalem, he kneeled upon his knees three times a day and prayed, and gave thanks before his God as he did aforetime. – **Daniel 6:10**

The Apostle Paul prayed daily too.

...that without ceasing I have remembrance of thee in my prayers night and day. – **2Timothy 1:3**

Prayer was the character, habit, and lifestyle of the Lord Jesus. He prayed in the morning, within the day, and at night.

And in the morning rising up a great while before day, he went out, and departed into a solitary place, and there prayed.

And it came to pass, as he was alone praying, his disciples were with him;

And it came to pass in those days, that he went out into a mountain to pray, and continued all night in prayer to God. – **Mark 1:35; Luke 9:18; Luke 6:12.**

Just like the men of old, as well as our Lord Jesus, our meeting with the Lord should be a daily affair and, at least twice daily – morning and evening. We become careless, therefore, when we, in one way or the other, neglect our daily communion with God.

"Prayer is the Christian's vital breath, the Christian's native air..."- **Angus Morrison**

Chapter 10

Toying with the Spirit of Worship

Worship is an essential aspect of prayer, it is as important in meaningful prayer as grease and oil are to the working of the moving parts of a machine.

Prayer, like I said earlier, is more than talking to God, it is talking with God. You can talk to a person who is either close to, or at some considerable distance from you.

However, talking with a person demands that the person be close to you. In fact, it requires the person to be with you right where you are.

Prayer in a very meaningful context will mean talking with God rather than talking to God.

If we must have and maintain a closer relationship and walk with God, we must completely do away with the mentality of talking to God far away in heaven and think about talking with Him right where we are. The earlier we do this, the better we will understand what nearness to God implies.

But, if we are to talk with God, He must be present with us, because, without His abiding and awesome presence, we cannot talk with Him.

Nothing else best ushers in the presence of God like worship. Worship moves God. Worship carries

God. Worship is the only comfortable environment of God. God and worship are two inseparable friends. Where there is true worship, worship in the spirit, there also is the presence of God.

If you find it difficult to give the presence of God an invitation, invite worship and worship will invite His presence. It is such an invitation that strengthens visitation.

Good knowledge of what worship is and how we should worship God, will help our prayer lives take on a new dimension.

The spirit of worship is dying-out in many congregations today and consequently in many lives.

Many of us most often look at worship in terms of "thanks-giving." Well, worship is not just thanksgiving, but includes it.

Thanksgiving is an expression of our gratitude to God, most especially for His mercy, kindness, and love towards us; and for everything, we believe He has done for us. It is simply an expression of our appreciation.

But that is not all about worship, anyway. There are two levels in the worship of God; gratitude and excellence. Dr. George Watson says that *"most people never get beyond the level of gratitude; and few worship God for His excellence, for all that He is, for His transcendent and immanent glory."*

This should not be so. We must worship God for His excellence and not only in gratitude. When we worship God in an expression of His excellence, we are talking about Who He is, how Great He is, how Incomparable He is.

We adore His Holiness. We tell Him how much we love Him and how much we treasure His presence.

We let Him know that there is no place that we would rather be than at His feet. We praise Him for His patience. We adore and magnify His Name for His works - His creation - the wonders of His hands.

We appreciate His Being: the Omnipotent, the Omnipresent, and the Omniscient.

Thus, when we worship God, we must let Him know that we love Him, not just because of all that He has done for us, but that, even if He did not do those things with which we appreciate Him, we would still love Him.

Therefore, in worship, we put behind the veil, ourselves, our situations, circumstances, successes, failures, achievements, pains, and everything else, just to give our utmost for His Highest.

We must learn to worship God deeply for His immanence and transcendence before 'flowing' into gratitude which is often expressed in thanksgiving.

When David worshipped the Lord in Psalms 104, he showed a practical example of what worship entails:

Bless the LORD, O my soul. O LORD my God, thou art very great; thou art clothed with honour and majesty. Who coverest thyself with light as with a garment: who stretchest out the heavens like a curtain:

Who layeth the beams of his chambers in the waters: who maketh the clouds his chariot: who walketh upon the wings of the wind: Who maketh his angels spirits; his ministers a flaming fire:

This is worship; worship that ushers in His Divine presence.

We too, invoke the warmth of God's presence, when we worship Him in the spirit and use words like, *You that walk upon the waters, the Mighty One in battle, the fourth man in the fire, with Eyes as of flaming fire, and Feet as fine brass. The only God with a thundering voice as of many waters, and with Whose release of breath, the earth lie bare.* ...

This is what true worship, worship in the spirit means.

Now, worship demands brokenness. The Bible implores us to worship Him in spirit. A time of worship is a time we should lift up holy hands to heaven and tell the Lord how much we love Him, and let the tears flow.

Today, people worship God dancing to the music of a worship song with dry hearts and open eyes. While others worship in utmost brokenness, they keep their eyes open, looking left and right, as if to say, *"We are waiting to see God descend so we might arrest Him."*

When you keep your eyes open and sing and dance during worship, what will you do during praises?

You see friend, worship should be an integral part of your prayer life. When you want to get into praying, you should give yourself time to catch up with the spirit of worship.

There are days you will wake up with a worshipful spirit and worshipful heart. There are also times you will need to start by taking one or two songs to worship the Lord. Sometimes, it may look difficult and dry, but you have to persist until you have a breakthrough into the spirit realm by continuing in heartfelt worship songs.

It is very necessary for you to worship the Lord and have a breakthrough if you must speak with the Lord, and of course if His Spirit must speak with you. For it is the Spirit of God Who tells you the mind of God in the presence of God.

For what man knoweth the things of a man, save the spirit of man which is in him? Even so the things of God knoweth no man, but the Spirit of God. **1Corinthians 2:11**

We become careless in prayer when we begin to toy with worship. It is rather better to spend time and worship the Lord with yet a heavy heart filled with needs than spend time asking and requesting from Him with little or no worship.

Worship is the grease of a prayer life. Toying with worship is toying with your prayer life, and through such carelessness creeps in spiritual dryness.

"Worship is the fastest Divine-transport that brings God's presence where you need Him when you need Him."

Chapter 11

Concord with the Spirit of Procrastination

The spirit of procrastination is the spirit of "I'll do it later."

The spirit of procrastination is the devil's legal adviser at a time when a prayer warrior gets the devil confused. 'He' is the devil's chief messenger to help a man reach a conclusion that is trying to decide whether to pray now or pray later.

'Do it later,' he'll say. 'Can you not see how tired and disorganized you are? By the way, you do not feel like praying, why force yourself? Why act against your will? See how unconducive the atmosphere is. Do it later!"

If you have never heard this spirit speak, many of us, have.

Here you are in the middle of the dark and quiet night awakened to pray by the Holy Spirit. Looking at the time, it is about 15 minutes past 1 A.M. You spend 5 good minutes trying to consider whether to pray now or pray later.

Before the next tick of the second hand of the clock, you hear a voice as simple as that of your spirit, speaking something in agreement with your body's desire at that time:

"If you pray now, what will you do by 4.am? Could it be the Holy Ghost that woke you up? If He is the One, what does He want you to pray for, now? Could the

Holy Spirit contradict the Word of God? Does it not say, 'He gives His loved ones sleep?' Have you forgotten you prayed before you slept? Must you die in prayer? Don't you even think the time you are using to think now is a waste, because you could have slept some far? It is better you stop pondering and sleep, so you can wake up early and have your quiet time."

This is where your trouble begins. Your sleeping at that time is concord with the spirit of procrastination and a disagreement with the Spirit of God.

When you postpone prayer, you sign a dangerous agreement with the devil which you have not taken time to read and understand the irreversible consequences and regrettable repercussions involved.

On the other hand, there is the spirit of prayer. When it comes upon you, all it says is 'pray' or 'go and pray.' You may not actually know what to pray for until you obey the command and go to pray.

And I will pour upon the house of David, and upon the inhabitants of Jerusalem, the spirit of grace and of supplications. – **Zechariah 12:10**

The spirit of procrastination is the greatest enemy of the spirit of prayer. If you take a stand with one, the other departs.

Have you ever experienced that when you have a burning desire to pray, the desire later dies slowly and perhaps completely if you decide to postpone it? And you may never pray again!

The simple truth is that you have taken a stand with the spirit of 'I'll do it later' and the spirit of prayer departs. Even if you later pray, the experience may not be the same as what it would have been if you did it at the right time.

"The fact that you do a thing later does not mean that it is the right time to do it." **Ntia I. Ntia**

We become careless in prayer when we agree with the spirit of 'I'll do it later'. If the spirit of procrastination tells you, "It is better you pray later," I think the right question you should often ask is, "What is wrong about my praying now?" You must learn to maintain your integrity.

That time of prayer the devil is telling you to postpone may be the right time for you to do the right praying for the right thing to happen. Carelessness in prayer through procrastination is a sure way of embracing spiritual dryness, which you may not be able to account for when it occurs.

"Anyone that marries procrastination ends up having regret and difficulty as children."

Chapter 12

Disdaining the Prayer Burden

Having a burden is another essential aspect of prayer. It is truly true that the secret of true praying is praying in the secret. But it is truer that the secret of praying in the secret is praying with a secret burden placed upon secret supports in the secret place of the heart.

Without a burden in the heart, it is difficult to pray from the heart. And prayer that is not from the heart may succeed in raising a dust of problems which will eventually resettle, but not move mountains.

A heart of prayer is a heart of burden. The truly praying person is a burden carrier. Burden is as essential to true and effective praying as fuel is to the effective working of a car. Burden is the fuel of prayer. Trying to pray without a burden is like trying to drive a car without fuel.

Burden is the only language our human spirit uses to interact with the Holy Spirit. Praying without a burden is like sleeping in Gethsemane.

Hear this! You will not be able to pray for the church until you have a burden for the church.

You will never pray for unbelieving men until you have a burden for their perishing souls.

You will never be able to pray for the salvation of your family until you have a burden for them.

You will never satisfactorily pray for your health, academics, work, and in fact anything, until there is a burden in your heart. That's why we cry often, 'Lord, give me a burden!'

"As a matter of fact," "Watchman Nee says, "we are not able to pray beyond our burden."

Burdens come from God. There are burdens, which originate within the prayer closet, and there are others, which God gives outside the closet.

When we are in the closet and the Holy Spirit gives a burden, it simply says, 'pray,' but a burden given outside the closet either says, 'rise up and pray,' or' 'go and pray.'

The 'pray' burden gets lighter in intensity in the prayer closet as we fervently pray, until it is no more, for the Lord lifts it off our hearts. As of then, we would have such an assuring witness that we have prayed and prayed through.

If, in any case, we try to pray a little for a heavy burden placed upon our heart in the prayer closet, we will eventually end the prayer in dissatisfaction, and find no peace in going ahead to pray for other things.

You see, a burden is like placing heavy logs of wood on a man's head with the instruction that, he should put them down one after the other. The more logs he puts to the ground, the lighter and more relieved he feels. But he is not completely relieved until he has put down the last log on his head.

Carrying that final log around will bring a feeling of uneasiness and discomfort until he puts it down.

This is exactly how a burden is. We may pray and really pray but the Lord may not be through with the lifting process. When it is finally done, we do not need to be told, as it will be evident by the satisfaction we will experience within.

There are burdens which God puts on us in the prayer closet and a ten minutes fervent prayer will get them lifted. But there are also burdens placed on us in the prayer closet which will lead us to spending hours, and perhaps, more than half a day in the presence of God.

Many men of God who have experienced this, will, if asked, tell us that they never envisaged staying that long in many instances they had such experiences. And whether we do expect to stay that long or not, God expects us to pray until the burdens are lifted.

Carelessness in prayer takes place when we begin to play with a God-given burden. In many cases, we substitute a short prayer for a heavy burden. We try to hurry over and pray for other needs. This is wrong.

We should remember that God is not man, and the Bible says He knows our needs before we call.

Where are we hurrying to?

Has God never blessed us with things we never prayed for? Has He never given us things we did not ask for?

We must understand that God goes beyond giving us what we ask for, and gives us even the desires of our heart, which we do not ask for. There is no need trying to force ourselves to tell Him everything when the time is limited. He knows how we feel.

Trying to hurry over a burden in prayer is carelessness in prayer and leads to spiritual dryness. This is because we do not only suppress the burden, but we disrupt the discussion between our spirit and the Spirit of God.

If we continue in that manner, we cast off the spiritual sensitivity that comes with a burden when we get into the closet. And that is where spiritual dryness again creeps in.

That was the 'pray' burden.

Now, the 'go and pray' burden comes upon you outside the prayer closet. Quite contrary to the 'pray' burden, it increases in intensity in your heart and spirit as you approach the closet, and finally gets to the peak when you enter the prayer closet.

It can come upon you in the office, in the school, at work, in the market, when you are with friends, etc. Wherever it comes, its command is as simple as, 'go and pray.' And you may not know what to pray for, until you go and begin praying.

Once this burden comes upon you, it makes you a changed person. Everything around you changes, including your behavior. There are certain things you won't be able to say, even in the midst of Christian friends.

You may be in a place where someone is so funny and everybody just laughs but you may not be able to do so. A sharp and observant person may likely ask if there is something wrong with you. In such instances, you may manage to forge a smile just to let the person believe all is well.

There is a stirring on the inside that you cannot understand until you get to the mountaintop. That is the 'go and pray' burden.

It was the 'go and pray' burden that moved the Lord Jesus towards Gethsemane.

And they came to a place which was named Gethsemane...and he taketh with him Peter and James and John, and began to be sore amazed, and to be very heavy;

and saith unto them, my soul is exceedingly sorrowful unto death... - **Mark 14:32-34**

It is extremely dangerous to despise this burden to pray. It is rather better to hurt friends and owe them an apology or explanation than hurt the Spirit of God to please friends, brethren, or family.

If any man come to me, and hate not his father, and mother, and wife and children and brethren, and sisters, yea, and his own life also, he cannot be my disciple. **–Luke 14:26**

It is extreme spiritual carelessness to sacrifice the prayer burden on the altar of distractions and busy schedules.

Can you pay the price of grieving the Spirit of God?

If the house or where you are in is not conducive, go to a conducive place. Oswald J. Smith sometimes prayed in the woods. William Bramwell agonized for some thirty-six hours in a sandpit. Father Nash, many times, buried his face in his hands in an agony of soul, right out in the woods. Jesus took a stroll down to Gethsemane. You, too, can stroll down somewhere.

Do not let the stirring die. Don't get the burden suppressed. It is carelessness in prayer, which leads to spiritual dryness.

"The secret of every spiritual decay is the decay of secret praying." – Gbile Akanni

Chapter 13

Trusting in Yesterday

Trusting in yesterday's prayer or yesterday's anointing is another aspect of carelessness in prayer.

Trusting in yesterday's prayer or anointing is like trusting in a shadow. Yesterday is gone and no more will be.

That Moses' face shone yesterday when he descended from the mountaintop does not mean it will forever shine while he remains in the camp.

How many hours did you spend praying yesterday? Can that be transferred to serve as a substitute for the prayerlessness of today? Can the long number of hours spent in the presence of God yesterday fill the vacancy created by today's relapse?

No Friend! This is where we fail and ignorantly fail. God demands some form of maturity in our reasoning if we must get close to His heart.

Now, think about it: can you eat some large pots of food today in order not to be hungry tomorrow? Of course, no! Whether you eat a plate, pot, or perhaps bags of food, once today is past it becomes yesterday, and yesterday is as gone as a broken egg.

Yesterday, no matter its anointing, fire, shower, power, and refreshment experienced is like a dead and buried hero which may yet be remembered, but has no more power to do anything, other than that which has already been done.

You may have fasted and prayed yesterday; you may have experienced some glory and some fire yesterday. And you may be tempted today to think of the experiences of that wonderful yesterday as though you can live in it and make today a spiritual holiday.

Well, we do not live in our yesterday. The glory of yesterday came yesterday for yesterday.

One of the greatest temptations a man of prayer can face is the temptation to believe today will always be like yesterday.

Trusting in yesterday is like looking back and praising yourself for how far you have gone in a long journey when you have only taken a step or two from the starting point.

The distance to where God wants us to be in our relationship with Him is twice farther than what we have already travelled and experienced. We have gone so far yet we are thousands of miles from where we are going.

No matter how much you prayed yesterday, it has nothing to do with today's prayer. No matter how much you pray today, it has nothing to do with tomorrow's prayer; hence the song, 'Yesterday's gone, today I'm in need.'

The earlier and better we understand this, the less our struggle to get closer to God and yet get nowhere will be.

We become careless in prayer when we begin to believe in the frequency of yesterday's prayer and perhaps try to live in the experience past. The opportunity of today's touch missed in God's presence by trusting in yesterday is like a treasure thrown into the deep sea.

And, a decision to glory in yesterday's glory is a decision to look away from, and despise the greater glory of today. It is another aspect of carelessness in prayer that culminates in spiritual dryness.

"Breathe on me, Holy Ghost power...yesterday's gone, today I'm in need..." – Clint Brown

Chapter 14

Prayer and Activity

Prayer cannot be substituted for activity. We must understand that it is a great necessity to have God work on us in order to have us walk with Him and work for Him.

The basic truth is that, if we must successfully work for Him, He must first work on us.

It is difficult for God to accept the services of a person He does not accept. In other words, for Him to accept our services, He must first accept our person. He must accept us first.

We should always consider the familiar story of Cain and Abel in the fourth chapter of Genesis. Why was Abel's sacrifice accepted and Cain's rejected? Did God accept the person of Cain? How could a gift whose giver is not accepted be accepted? Was this not God's immediate response to Cain's anger?

If thou doest well, shall thou not be accepted? – **Genesis 4:7**

God did not say, "Shall thy gift not be accepted?" but said, "Shall thou not be accepted?" Of course, the person of the giver matters more to God than his gift or offering. Thus, the one rendering the service matters more to Him than the service rendered.

There are too many people who exert and wear themselves out to work for a

God Who neither knows nor accepts them. We must be conscious enough of His acceptance of our person before we ever think of our service to Him. This demands such a wonderful closeness to Him.

If this is so, we must cherish above all else, our closets. For, where else are we better fashioned than in the secret place? Where else are we better shaped to fit into the work than when alone with Him?

We, sometimes, spend so much time working for God without knowing that we have walked out of step with Him. We must, therefore, develop the attitude of a heart-to-heart talk with Him, so we can let Him point to us where we have derailed without the least knowledge.

If we do not constantly hear from Him the way He will have us do the work, we may serve amiss and like Uzzah, bear the consequence of supporting the falling ark, when He would not want us to do that.

Any activity then, which deprives us of the opportunity to constantly speak with God, only soon, renders us useless and 'good-for-nothing.'

"Every servant of God must spend much more time on his face before God than he ever does in the work God gives him to do." - Rebecca **Brown.**

Chapter 15

Prayer Needs Fasting

Prayer needs fasting for its development. Fasting is the boost of a prayer life. It is the 'life' of a prayer life. It is the energy supplier of the soul and the power elevator of the spirit.

We actually grow in our prayer life. And this 'growth in prayer' phenomenon is really a continuous process. Fasting is the fertilizer that enhances the growth of the prayer life. Some do not fast and so do not grow. Rather than daily progress spiritually, they regress.

Failure in fasting is also failure in prayer. Carelessness with fasting is carelessness with prayer. A Christian will be poorer spiritually and his prayer life will never be what God wants it to be until he practices the privilege of fasting.

Most believers practice 'fasting procrastination' instead of fasting. "I'll fast tomorrow," they'll always say. When tomorrow comes, they make a new decision to fast tomorrow. And unfortunately, every *tomorrow* comes except the *tomorrow* of the fast. They live in procrastination, which is a big spiritual indiscipline. A true disciple of Jesus Christ is a disciplined follower.

You may never fast if you are one of those that wait for God to tell you to fast before you do so. Regular habits of fasting and prayer should be a natural part of your spiritual life.

Fasting is to prayer what the file is to a cutlass. A blunt and carefree life of fasting makes a blunt and careless life of prayer. This then eventuates in spiritual dryness.

"Carelessness in fasting is voluntary retirement from the possession of spiritual power."

Chapter 16

Carelessness in the Study of the Word

The truly praying Christian is the one who truly, carefully, and painfully studies the Word of God. We pray in what we study. And without an effective study of the Word, we pray amiss.

We talk with God in prayer and God speaks to us through His Word. Our obedience to God depends on how much we hear from Him. We cannot dream of obeying a God we do not hear from. His Word is our compass and our lamp. It is what directs us in the midst of strange darkness.

Thy word is a lamp unto my feet, and a light unto my path. - **Ps 119:105**

The Word is the food of your soul. Neglecting to study the Word is neglecting to feed your soul.

My soul thirsts for the living God. – **Psalms 42:2**

The soul cannot do without the Word, as it embodies the mind. If the mind must be constantly renewed (Ephesians 4:23); if we must have a fresh mental and spiritual attitude, we must constantly feed the soul with the Word.

We are not just to read the Word, we are to study it. We are to dig deep into it, and "*Study to show ourselves approved unto God.*"

Take a look at two insects: the butterfly and the bee. Both insects love flowers. But look at the butterfly. It jumps from flower to flower and spends no time on any of them. It gathers no pollen and sucks no nectar. Maybe this is the reason the butterfly looks lighter and relatively harmless.

Take a close look at the bee. It is quite different. It selects a flower, sits on it, and puts out its proboscis and there it will sit for minutes drawing all the nectar and gathering all the pollen found there. When it has gathered enough, off it flies.

With the nectar and pollen, it can feed both itself and its children. The bee then, looks heavier in structure and has the ability to deal with anybody that tries to play over its intelligence.

When we become careless with the Word of God, jump from place to place in it, from book to book, from chapter to chapter, without actually settling down to grasp what God has for us in a particular portion, we become like the butterfly. And we become lighter and harmless to the kingdom of Satan.

It is the Word of God that spurs us up to pray. It is the Word that teaches us what to pray for. It is the Word that provides the faith we need to receive from God. It is the Word that actually energies our spirit and sets it on fire for prayer.

Negligence of the Word is negligence of prayer. Carelessness in the study of the Word is Carelessness in prayer, and carelessness in both implies multiple preparations to usher in spiritual dryness.

"It is impossible to be strong in prayer if we are not strong in the Scripture." – Ernest J. Gruen.

Chapter 17

Lack of Fruitful Study of the Word

An aspect of carelessness in the study of the Word is the lack of fruitful study of it. There is no better avenue God reveals Himself to us than through His Word. A desire to know more of God is a desire to know more of His Word.

A deep desire to get closer to God begins with a deep desire to study His Word. A deep longing for the Word is the beginning of a deeper love for the Lord.

... If a man loves me, he will keep my words: and my Father will love him, and

we will come unto him, and make our abode with him. **John 14:23**

One of the events of greatest value in our daily routine should be the study of the Word: sitting at it to fathom the depth of its truth.

Do you know that there is a deeper truth in the verse you just read this morning? Do you know that there is a greater revelation in the verse you just read past?

The Word is deeper than the depth we know, and there are deeper truths in the truth we know. The problem is that we are sometimes too busy to sit down and be taught of the Spirit. We, therefore, always end up scratching the surface and yet get nothing, because the riches lie deep beneath the surface.

It is better we settle down and study a verse of Scripture and fathom the truth embedded within than read thousands of verses with a spiritual understanding and enlightenment about nothing.

No man is too knowledgeable to study the Word. There is the deepest spiritual wisdom embedded in the portion anyone would feel he has already acquired all. Claiming to have studied enough of the Word is like claiming to have emptied an ocean with a small glass cup. The deepest revelation we think we have is most often, the beginning of our journey into where the deepest lies.

That is why, backsliding after we have been Christians for many years and thereafter claiming to have known enough of the Word, is as deceptive as thinking we can breathe and empty the air in the whole world in a lifetime. We may have gone so far in the eyes of men, but as far as not having started in the eyes of God.

Carelessness in the study of the Word begins when we sit at it for short or long periods without having any fruitful study in the least. Then, we leave as empty as we came, feeling satisfied from an understanding of nothing.

This is very dangerous. It is like being so much in need of water that you let down an empty bucket deep into a well of water, and bring it out with a feeling of satisfaction but cannot find even a drop of water inside.

You see, among other things, God will always want to expose our depravity and helplessness in the light of His Word as we study at His feet with a quiet, gentle, and patient spirit, no matter the level of our relationship with Him.

Such an experience is what we should greatly seek after as we approach His presence to study at His feet.

Also, He will always want to show us how much He can help our helplessness and how much He can transform our depraved nature, and fill us with all of His fullness (Ephesians 3:19).

He will always reveal to us that the greatest we can do and the best we can accomplish without Him is nothing, thereby revealing His Omnipotence and providence, and our impotence and helplessness.

We may not be studying the Word at all, if we do not have these experiences. God desires that these should be daily experiences for us if we must taste the greatness of His immanent and transcendent glory.

Treating such experiences with levity is an indication that we are unwilling to pay the price of closeness to Him.

You may be asking, "How long should we spend studying the Word?" Well, the answer is so simple and straightforward, I think. It is not how long we sit at the Word that matters, but how well we study it when we sit at it.

The amount of time spent in a fruitful study of the Word is just the right amount of time that should be given to studying it. And any fruitful study of the Word should always bring to our hearts a revelation of the Lord Himself; His Glory, as well as His Holiness, Greatness, Love, and power; and at the same time expose or bring to light our own depravity, impotence, and helplessness.

Sitting to study the Word at any time without such a focus and desire, is carelessness in the study of the Word which eventually becomes a trail to our prayer lives in particular and our relationship with God in general.

No matter what height we have attained, we still need to daily cry like the psalmist: *Open thou mine eyes that I may behold wondrous things out of thy law,* and sing like the songwriter: 'Teach me Lord to understand all the glory, all the beauty of your love,' lest we become careless and unconsciously invite spiritual dryness into our lives. For, the greatest height we have attained is but thousands of miles below where God will have us be.

In the light of this truth, we should individually ask: When last did I have a fruitful study of the Word?

"A closer walk with the Lord begins with a deeper walk in the Word."

Chapter 18

Neglect of Study of the Word

Neglect of the Word for a day or more is another serious aspect of carelessness in the study of the Word.

A.W. Tozer wrote, "Whatever keeps me from the Bible is my enemy, however harmless it may appear to be. Let the cares of life crowd out the Scriptures from my mind and I have suffered loss where I can least afford it."

When we neglect to study the Word, we neglect a revelation. There are too many things to know about God in this short life for us to miss a day's revelation. There is so much in the throne-room for us to know about God that even if we lived a thousand years we would not even fathom the least.

"Often when we kneel in prayer, the lost years cry out behind us," wrote David Macintyre. Our life is too short to miss such a great privilege we are given daily to know and experience a God too great to be described as great.

The best of our closeness to Him may only be an experience of a little of Who He is, and the best we know of Him may only be the smallest portion of less than little of Who He really is. But we know that He is willing to unravel more of Who He is to us as we daily study at His Feet with the willingness to obey.

I think the best desire we can have is that of the Apostle Paul, who after experiencing all the riches and fantasies of this world and then the power of God in man, yet cried fervently: *"That I may know Him!"*

Our problem begins the day we neglect to study the Word.

Whose despiseth the word shall be destroyed. –**Proverbs 13:13**

What an offer of nothing we receive for such a high price we pay.

Could we ever live a better life than the life of God in man?

Could we have a better day than the day we hear Him speak?

Could there be any close substitute in value for a day's revelation in the Word missed?

I doubt!

But in case there may be, the closest substitute will be as far from the value of a revelation as the days of man compared to that of God.

There is also the Spirit of truth. He is the Teacher of the Word; the One we should call unto for help as we sit to study the Word. He is the life in the Word. He often goes beyond bearing witness with our spirit that we are God's sons, to quickening the Truth of God's Word in our spirit man.

....For He will take from what is Mine and will declare it to you. – **John 16:14** *(Berkeley Version)*

We cannot do without the Holy Spirit if we must have a fruitful study of the Word; for, "*the letter kills but the Spirit gives life.*" The earlier we know to pray:

'*Come thou Spirit of truth, that the truth I may know,*' the more we will experience His glory through the Word.

Trying to study the Word without the help of the Spirit is as fatal as completely neglecting to study the Word. We must know that every part of the Scripture must be studied in the Spirit in which it was written.

Imagine a Christian, so much in a hurry that he just manages to glance into a portion of the Bible. Yesterday, he read a few verses, and tomorrow he may never look into it at all.

Glancing at the Word when we are already in a haste is as good as not opening it at all, because the Spirit cannot come running after us. It is as good as a complete neglect. This is how we allow spiritual dryness to creep in unnoticed.

It is not as though reading the Word without really studying it at a particular time is wrong, no-not at all. But, we ought to have time to sit at His Feet daily and study without mistaking it with mere reading.

Have you ever neglected to study the Word for one day? How did you feel about it? Did you ever think about the price you paid? Do you know that each day is a vessel to be loaded with holy deeds and earnest endeavours before it sets sail for the eternal shores?

Have you ever found anything else that could well fill the vacancy created by the revelation you missed? Do you not think such a degree of carelessness in the study of the Word is too high?

Could what you are neglecting not be the same thing that keeps you? Think about it.

"Revelations in the Word quickened into our spirit are the footprints of God in the pathways of our life. What a great price we pay when we neglect a day!"

Please note this if you are a preacher: It is dangerous to always sit studying the Word just to teach or preach to others. It is carelessness of a sort to always spend time studying to teach others and never teaching ourselves.

You see, only a broken man can break men. If the Word does not break us, it may be difficult to break others. Others we teach or preach to may not have any good encounter with the

Word if we have not had such encounters in the least.

The best person we can ever preach to is ourselves. The greatest corrections we may need to give, may be to ourselves. There may always be traces in us of what we try to condemn in others.

It is true that the easiest thing to find is a fault, but how easy it is to find it lying carelessly on the veranda of someone else's character than ours! We become so longsighted that we can see all the ills that need to be corrected in others without being able to see our very own.

I am afraid we may be exposing our weakest weakness each time we try to impatiently reprimand the weaknesses and frailties of others. If there is anyone we should be afraid of, it is ourselves, and if there is anything to fear it is our own heart.

It is not wrong to study so we can teach or preach to others, but we need to have a good deal of what we want others to benefit from in the venules and capillaries of our own soul.

If we constantly search the Scriptures during our quiet time for the purpose of preaching to or teaching others, we may soon be dying from a need of what we are giving to others.

If we always go to God with the mind of *taking to give*, we may be playing the part of a carpenter who is so busy making doors for others that he cannot make even one for himself and, therefore, lives in a house without doors.

It is possible to be the best teacher of what we cannot do. It is also possible to preach the truth in the best manner possible and live contrary to it.

We may live the worst lives on earth if we cannot allow what we teach others to send down roots in us. The simplest things we teach others to observe may be the hardest things for us to do.

And sometimes, we may actually be condemning ourselves in our best messages to others.

I think the best we can do is sit at the Lord's Feet, and like David cry, 'Search me O God', and then cry, 'Master please break me!' Else, how can we reveal the frailties in others if we overlook ours?

Could the Prophet Hosea have ever understood the level of Israel's prostitution in her relationship with God better than being married to prostitute?

Could the Prophet Isaiah ever have much to say about the unholiness of others if he did not realize his hellishness before God?

How can we best explain to the ignorant, the difficulty or simplicity of a process we have never been through?

I think we can best explain the breaking and remolding power of God only if we have visited the potter's house. We can talk best to others about His Glory if we have been at the Mount of Transfiguration with Him.

Our failure today lies in the fact that we try to explain an experience to others, which we have never experienced. We try to burden others with burdens we have never carried. We try to lead others to places we have never been before – what a costly confusion!

Let us have a good grasp of the Word and we will be able to let others have it. Let us have a fountain of the Word, and others will benefit from its overflow. We need to have some life to be able to help the lifeless.

Spiritual dryness will always creep in when we forget to remember that the axe-head was borrowed. It is an extreme form of carelessness in the study of the Word when we constantly search through it only to enrich others, while we languish in spiritual poverty.

"We may live the worst lives on earth if we cannot allow what we teach others send down roots in us."

Chapter 19

Carelessness in the Use of the Tongue

Carelessness in the use of the tongue is one of the surest ways of running into spiritual dryness. Most often, we engage in certain discussions and arguments which are very ungodly and unedifying in outcome.

But keep away from those godless, empty discussions, for they lead people further on into godlessness. - **2 Timothy 2:16** *(Berkeley version)*

How do we become careless in the use of our tongue?

But I say unto you, That every idle word that men shall speak, they shall give account thereof in the day of judgment.   Matt 12:36

As children of God, we often at one time or the other find ourselves in conversations we ought not to engage in. We often, as Christians, drift into idle and hurtful conversations in an attempt to entertain or sound pleasant.

Our words are supposed to be timely. An idle word is a word with no specific purpose and direction. It is spoken for speaking sake. It is spoken carelessly, and like a bullet once released can never be recalled.

Our words – whether able or idle – are seeds sown in the lives of others. Able words are powerful positive words, but most idle words are negative. Positive words make great listeners, but negative words mar them.

Positive words are right words spoke at the right time. They have creative abilities in others. Negative words never have a right time, for the time is never right to say the wrong thing. Negative words bring hurt, condemnation, and curses. They create disability in the spiritual lives of others. When we speak negatively we merely equip the devil to act. This is very dangerous.

Sometimes, we just speak out of a desire to crack jokes, but we end up realizing that we cracked jokes that turned out to be a trail to our spiritual lives. Some things we say in form of Jokes turn out, many times, to war against our souls.

We should learn that the tongue is an outlet of power. Many of us get blessed and filled with God's fullness, but it all runs out through the tongue. Let us learn to say nothing when we have nothing to say. When we speak idly, we merely try to say something out of nothing. But how often dangerous this is!

Someone who is sure of himself does not talk all the time – **Proverbs 17:27** (Good News Version)

We should not talk because we feel like talking. Jesus was the Greatest Economist of Words. He spoke only relevant words when they were relevant; and, "*to such experience you have been called; that you might follow in His footsteps*"(1Peter 1:21). Talking idly is becoming careless with the tongue.

"An idle word degrades the personality of a noble speaker."

Chapter 20

When We Talk Too Much

The more you talk, the more likely you are to sin. If you are wise you will keep quiet. – **Proverbs 10:19** *(Good News Version)*

"*A talkative person is a sinner,*" observed a writer. And "*a talkative person cannot be a prophet,* " Dr. D.K. Olukoya adds.

Many times we become too talkative as Christians. And the more we talk with men, the less we talk with God. This is the more reason why we most often spend as much as two hours talking with each other but less than thirty minutes talking with God.

The greater stirred the appetite to talk with men, the more dampened the appetite to talk with God. The more concerned we are with the external, the less control we have over the internal.

Sometimes, when we engage in long-term conversations, we are bound to exaggerate at one point or the other or tell a lie backed with regret on the inside of us somewhere. And many times, we get pushed either by the form or nature of our conversation to consciously or unconsciously speak evil of someone else within or without the Christian fold, thereby grieving the Holy Spirit. Oh, how unpeaceful and destabilized we soon become within!

We are supposed to be swift to hear and slow to speak. But we rather seem to be swift to speak and slow to hear.

We talk more than we hear, rather than hear more than we talk. And when we dare to talk too much about ourselves, our abilities, achievements, or attainments, we find a little boast, a little expression of pride, and a little exaggeration in the face of praises. By the time we finish talking, all the 'littles' during our little long talk have formed a big wall of partition between us and God.

Let us, therefore, learn to talk little about what we see ourselves to be, and learn to give God the praise for what He has made us. Let us learn to talk less to men about ourselves and talk more to them about Jesus.

Let us learn to talk less with men about wrong situations and unwanted circumstances in the home, school, office, church, etc., and talk much with God about them. For, we will often unlikely, gossip the people or situations we pray for; just as we unlikely pray for the situations or people we gossip.

Talking too much is being careless with the tongue. It leads to loss of virtue, spiritual savor, and consequently, spiritual dryness.

Wherefore, my beloved brethren, let every man be swift to hear, slow to speak... **James 1:19**

"Excessive talking is a sure indication of someone whose heart is not composed." – Derek Prince

When We Speak Without Grace

It is the grace of God that first works in the heart to bring salvation. This should be the most reason salvation is termed the first work of grace.

For the grace of God that bringeth salvation..... **Titus 2:11**

After salvation, the same grace dwells in the heart to accomplish other works, one of which is sanctification. It is this grace within, that teaches that *"denying ungodliness and worldly lusts, we should live soberly, righteously, and godly, in this present world"* (Titus 2:12).

It is this same store of grace in the heart that affects the believer's speech, language, or words, so that when he sings or worships the Lord, it is not with a forceful, mechanical struggle, but *"with grace in his heart to the Lord"* (Colossians 3:16).

In the same manner, knowing that *"Out of the abundance of the heart the mouth speaks,*" the true believer's words are supposed to be saturated, supported, and brought out with grace at all times. This became the Apostle Paul's admonition to the Colossian Church:

Let your speech be always with grace....
Colossians 4:6

The word "always" implying "at all times" indicates that grace is, and should constantly be the natural environment of the believer's heart and subsequently, the nature of his words.

He really may, no doubt, be irritated, discouraged, or troubled by some situations, but if he is to speak, his words must be with grace. And, grace is that which goes with his speech and brings comfort, joy, happiness, consolation, encouragement, satisfaction, and cleansing to whoever he speaks to.

To the Church at Ephesus, the Apostle admonished:

Let no corrupt communication proceed out of your mouth, but that which is good to the use of edifying, that it may minister grace unto the hearers. **Ephesians 4:29**

The word 'edify' implies to improve someone else's life, spiritual character, or thought life. And the words "minister grace" have the import of "impart grace". As children of God, workers in His vineyard, leaders, or Ministers of the Gospel, could these be just what our words do? Or, do we ever speak words which neither edify nor bless?

Could we still be "ministering grace" to the hearers when we allow from us those foul, polluting, unwholesome, worthless, degrading languages, which we very often hear ourselves say?

Should we not have earlier learned from the Lord Jesus that it is *"that which cometh out of a man's mouth that defileth the man"* (Matthew 15:18)?

Should we not, by certain, have grown in Him to know that the filthy languages we use on each other in our little meetings, or on others by virtue of our offices and positions of responsibility in the Lord's vineyard, much more than pollute, defile, and demoralize such ones, does so the more to us?

Do we ever think about the result of such actions, or maybe we are just tempted to feel, "*Well, they have no spiritual implications. The Lord overlooks them.*"

Oh, how fatal that would be!

One of the results of our ungracious words is often spiritual dryness, as the sad and grieved Holy Spirit quietly withdraws.

I'd think in addition to the many things we know about the Holy Spirit, we also must know that though He is very good in making known and announcing His coming upon a life, He so silently withdraws when grieved.

That we see the anointing continually manifested and power consistently displayed is no proof that we are still in tune with Him! Such knowledge should help us consistently pray, *Pour out Thine grace much more into mine heart, Dear Lord, that my mouth, at all times, nothing else but grace may utter!"*

Some of us are very good at criticizing others. Anything that does not seem to look the way we think or done the way we want is at the mercy of our criticism.

I have realized in the course of my Christian life, that people who criticize things so easily are people that cannot do those things better if they were given the same opportunity.

A Christian that criticizes the Pastor or Minister in charge so much, is, or would likely be a very poor house fellowship leader.

Thomas A Kempis had said that *"If a man would weigh his own deeds fully and rightly, he would find little cause to pass severe judgment on others."*

Many a time, we find people in a Church criticizing a soloist or song leader for some common mistakes made in the course of singing. Get closer to them and you'll realize that if given a microphone and an opportunity to sing, they may make the same or worse mistakes.

"Destructive criticism is a job for the jobless person who is not willing to have a job. It is better to rise up and do something and be criticized by another than sit down and do nothing but criticize others."

Let us learn to appreciate the little others can do and then pray more for them rather than criticize them. When we criticize destructively, we speak without grace. We can learn to gently and graciously correct others.

The Lord Jesus said to His disciples, *"Now ye are clean through the word which I have spoken unto you"* (John 15:3), and by so doing laid a pattern for our speech.

Our words must have a purifying and cleansing power. They must be beneficial to the spiritual progress of others. They must have a building effect.

Spiritual dryness can result from our lack of self-control in the use of the tongue. Let us, therefore, be careful to give *"sound speech that cannot be condemned"* (Titus 2:8a).

"The words you speak will either put you over or hold you in bondage." – **Charles Capps**

Chapter 21

Carelessness in Companionship

Be not deceived; evil communications corrupt good manners. **-1Corinthians 15:33**

The caliber of people we walk with, talk with, and generally deal with, affect our Christian lives in one way or the other – if not positively, then negatively. The people we have as companions will either help to build us up or help to pull us down.

How is it that some Christians so enjoy the company of unbelievers? Most Christians retort, "I can stay with them. Whatever they say does not move me – at all."

Wow! What a lie!

Listen! What we hear affects us a lot. Whatever we hear has the power to build or destroy us on the inside. Faith cometh by hearing – yes! But fear also cometh by hearing!

Let us never feel so anointed to stay in the midst of unbelievers and listen to their immoral jesting, music, gossip, and backbiting, without being uncomfortable. The simple command is, "come out from among them."

"We think of what we hear and act the way we think."

Four Kinds of Friends

There are four categories of people that exist around us, just like we have four basic arithmetical signs. We have people that add, subtract, multiply, and divide us.

People That Add On (To) Us

These are people that come around us and exert a positive influence over our lives. When they come to us they seem to carry along some air of encouragement, progress, prayerfulness, and ministration. If they meet us at any time in a moody state, they know how to get us excited. If we have a vision, they know how to help bring it unto maturity. When the going seems tough, their attitudes teach us to look only at the positive, rather than the negative side of things. They help us bring our dreams to actualization and reality.

Each time such people are around us, they challenge us spiritually in one way or the other. Anytime we get close to them, we leave with a stirring on the inside to get closer to the Lord. They simply add on (to) us.

Watchman Nee in his own words related his experience with regard to this:

When I began to serve the Lord I was determined to do the will of God. Naturally I felt I have done His will. But whenever I went to see a certain sister to talk with her and to read some verses of the Bible together, I was immediately convinced of my inadequacy. Each time I saw her, I felt something special: God was there. By getting near to her you sensed God, for she had light, and her life was governed by God's light. As you come near to her, her light would convict you.

These are the kind of companions we must treasure in order to maintain a life of spiritual freshness. Iron sharpens iron, fire begets fire, and life begets life. The level of spiritual growth we attain is largely dependent on the spiritual attitude and level of closeness to God of the people we constantly share with. To grow, we must share with them that consistently grow.

"Life begets life!"

People That Subtract (From) Us

People that subtract from us are the exact opposite of those that add to us. They do not see what we see. Our visions and aspirations are a burden to them.

Each time we try to discuss anything about prayer, the Word of God, great Ministers of God, the anointing, and so on, they become very uncomfortable because, to them, we seem to be sounding too spiritual.

The Bible says, *"Their throats are open graves,"* meaning that whatever comes out of them is stinking, dirty, corrupt, and worthless.

The only things such people can talk about after a good church service is how the chorus leaders were dull; how the pastor preaches one message always, and that, without the anointing; and how a brother was looking at a sister with an evil intention.

Moreover, they acquire habits of idleness as they go around visiting homes, and not merely are they idle but they are gossips and busybodies, saying things they should not. - **1Timothy 5:13**

The Bible also says *the poison of asps is under their lips* (Romans 3:13). That means, no matter how joyful you are in the spirit, just a word from them dries it up.

If you dare share a progressive vision with them, the only contributions they offer will do no more than help thwart the vision.

Furthermore, they are people you get close to, and by the time you leave, your prayer life, as well as most other Christian virtues, are gone.

"One who is the companion of a believer with a spiritually subtractive attitude, simply shows the devil a shortcut into his life."

People that Multiply

These are people who have learnt to appreciate and encourage us in our little efforts. When we are wrong, they tell us that we are wrong. They praise us when we are right.

Even when we do not seem to perform well in a given situation, they do their best to encourage us: *"Oh, I never knew you could do that so well,"* they'll say. *"I was impressed."* These words multiply us. They increase our size on the inside. They propel us forward.

"Encouragement is the manure that helps our visions of greater spiritual attainment to grow."

People That Divide

This group occupies a greater portion numerically. Their work is to divide us. Even when we are wrong, they cannot boldly correct us, but will be bold enough to tell others about our mistakes and even paint it as though we have committed the greatest sin that perhaps, demands an eleventh commandment.

Beware, then, of a brother or sister who is always trying to divide others before you, while he or she tells you how perfect you are, because one day, you too will be divided in the presence of other people.

It is better to hear the reproof of the wise, than for a man to hear the song of fools. – **Ecclesiastes 7:5**

"A companion who divides others before you is the devil's tool for growing the crops that beae the fruits of hatred and bitterness against others in your heart."

Our Companionship Affects Our Spirituality

When we get close to worldly companions, we soon become like them. When we make friends with prayerless persons, we soon become prayerless too. And when we make friends with prayerful people, we get challenged to pray.

Deep calleth unto deep – **Psalms 42:7**

Friendship with an immoral fellow soon leads to immorality. And one who prefers to be close to a backslider soon becomes like him.

In fact, most of our sorrows, downfall, and spiritual degeneration, are results of wrong relationships and companionships. The less we associate with the wrong people, the better our lives become.

Worldly companionship is very dangerous. We cannot be of help to our fellowmen if we lower ourselves to their level. Worldliness leads to spiritual dryness.

What is worldliness? "Worldliness is anything that makes sin look attractive and righteousness look silly," a wise writer defined. We are worldly when we live and choose as people who do not love God.

Most believers in an effort to become modern Christians have become worldly Christians. Trying to walk, talk, dress, and act like the world can cause us to eventually go back to the things we left behind.

For if after they have escaped the pollutions of the world through the knowledge of the Lord and Saviour Jesus Christ, they are again entangled therein, and overcome, the latter end is worse with them than the beginning. For it had been better for them not to have known the way of righteousness, than, after they have known it, to turn from the holy commandment delivered unto them. **2Peter 2:20-21**

Immediately we begin to get comfortable with the things we once stood against, preached against, and frowned at, we must know that something is somehow wrong somewhere.

For if I build again the things which I destroyed, I make myself a transgressor. **Galatians 2:18**

The world is exceedingly worldly just as sin is exceedingly sinful. Worldliness is one of the major spiritual paths bearing the footprints of men that have been led to the territory of spiritual dryness.

In summary, therefore, success in our spiritual lives depends on whether we entangle with spiritually successful people or spiritual failures; whether we interact with people who daily overcome and grow in their relationship with God or spiritual dwarfs who live in daily defeats.

Dr. Paul Yonggi Cho says, "*By having wonderful fellowship with successful people, we can mutually encourage each other. People who fail always gather with others with their kind of failures. We should be careful in choosing our friends.*"

We should be able to do away with companions or friends who contribute nothing to our spiritual development and growth. What is the benefit we derive from having a Christian friend, who, each time he or she visits, sleeps all night while we pray, and eats all day while we fast?

Again, when we make friends with Christians who keep telling us, "It is not easy," it is probable that we too will soon see it as, "not easy," and get it all hard going, because what we see is what we get. But when we get close to spiritual champions, we get challenged and encouraged to attain greater heights.

Our companionship can be a gateway to great spiritual blessings, commitment, uplifting, and fulfillment, as well as great spiritual backwardness, mediocrity, and defilement depending on our choice of friends. Our companionship affects our spirituality, let us be wise!

Friendship with Jesus, Fellowship divine, Oh, what blessed sweet Communion, Jesus is a friend of mine (an old hymn).

"One who is careless in his companionship with men is careless about his relationship with God."

Chapter 22

Withdrawal from Fellowship

Withdrawal from fellowship can lead to a loss of spiritual freshness.

It is dangerous to stay away from a meeting in the Church or fellowship no matter how spiritually strong we think we are. There are certain blessings God will give us in our prayer closest, but there are others, which God can only give us where brethren are gathered together in His name. An example is found in Acts 2:1-4.

And when the day of Pentecost was fully come, they were all with one accord in one place. And suddenly there came a sound from heaven as of a rushing mighty wind, and it filled all the house where they were sitting. **Acts 2:1-2**

"When we are with God's people, we can be brought face to face with the love, power, and majesty of God." – **Reinhard Bonnke**

Most believers consider Bible studies to be less important. They believe they will receive all they want during the Miracle Services.

No! God wants us to learn and to know more about Him, daily. He is not only interested in our physical prosperity but also the prosperity of our soul. In fact, our prosperity in the physical is most often a manifestation of the prosperity of the soul.

Beloved, I wish above all things that thou mayest prosper and be in health, even as thy soul prospereth. **3 John 2**

From the above Scripture, it is easy to see that our prosperity in the physical is a result of the prosperity in the soul. Berkeley version puts it this way:

*Beloved friend, I pray that you may get along well in every way and may enjoy health **just as your soul is prospering.***

In other words, the Bible is saying, just as your soul is prospering, prosper also in the physical.

But the soul cannot prosper without the Word of God. That is why God told Joshua:

This book of the law shall not depart out of thy mouth; but thou shalt meditate therein day and night, that thou mayest observe to do according to all that is written therein: FOR THEN THOU SHALT MAKE THY WAY PROSPEROUS, AND THEN THOU SHALT HAVE GOOD SUCCESS. **- Joshua 1:8**

Bible studies in our churches or fellowships are very important. The Revival and Miracle Services are important too. Each of them is important in its peculiar way, and must also be treated as such. Being a Sunday-Sunday believer can be very dangerous.

Most believers use their businesses as an excuse for staying away from fellowship. Well, using our businesses to excuse ourselves is using them to accuse ourselves, because our businesses were made for us and not we for our businesses.

Not slothful in business; fervent in spirit; serving the Lord. – **Romans 12:11**

Most Christians become slothful in business so they can serve the Lord, while others are so hardworking in business but cannot serve the Lord. Both actions are wrong. The instruction is, *"not slothful in business; fervent in spirit."*

One of the reasons some of us are spiritually dry today is that we asked God to provide us with something to do and He granted our request, but we have become so busy in our work that we have forgotten Him.

'Oh, I'm just too tired to attend fellowship today,' we will always say.

"The little God makes us today is but a little test to see how we will treat our relationship with Him tomorrow

if He were to make us as great as His plan for us is. Yet, many of us have failed this test already."

Chapter 23

Cooperate Fellowship – Cooperate Anointing

*Now there were in the church that was at Antioch certain prophets and teachers;...As they ministered to the Lord, and fasted, the Holy Ghost said, separate me Barnabas and Soul for the work whereunto I have called them. – **Acts 13:1,2***

Barnabas and Saul (later named Paul) were called for a particular Ministry after they fasted and prayed and worshiped the Lord together. We will notice here that it was not when either Paul or Barnabas was fasting and praying alone that they were called.

I am not kicking against individual and personal fast here. But I, at the same time, believe it to be improper for a believer to absent himself or herself from fellowship because he or she is having a personal fast. I would rather feel it is better to go with the fast and fellowship with the other brethren because that could be another source of edification.

An old wise writer had given a warning which may benefit anyone that cares: *"Beware of indifference to community prayer through love of your own devotions."*

It is spiritually dangerous to operate with the principle of 'every man to himself and God to us all' in the Body of Christ.

"Worshipping God together with other believers is an essential part of

being a Christian. The Bible says nothing about solo believers." – Reinhard Bonnke

David's Example

We will recall that it was when David absented himself from warfare that he fell into immorality (adultery).

And it came to pass, after the year was expired, at the time when kings go forth to battle, that David sent Jaob and his servants with him, and all Israel; and they destroyed the children of Ammon, and besieged Rabbah. But David tarried still at Jerusalem. And it came to pass in an evening tide, that David arose from off his bed, and walked upon the roof he saw a woman washing herself; and the woman was very beautiful to look upon. And David sent messengers, and took her and she came in unto him, and he lay with her.

But the thing that David has done displeased the Lord. - **2Samuel 11:1,2,4, and 27b**

Now, David did not just absent himself from warfare and fall immediately. It took some steps. He sent others to go and fight while he stayed back.

Then, one evening he got up from his couch and walked upon the roof of the royal palace. At this time he must have been idle. And there is no set of people the devil loves like idle men.

The Apostle Paul wrote: *Warn the idle...* - **1Thessalonians 5:14**

Sometimes, when one is idle, he thinks, reasons and acts foolishly. The devil flashes a lot of things into his idle mind. The Bible says, from the roof, David saw – no other thing – but a naked woman taking her bath, and she was exceptionally beautiful. One step led to the other until he fell.

"An idle man is an idol to himself."

This is exactly what happens to us when we absent ourselves from fellowship for no just cause. Step by step we lose our spiritual freshness. It is, therefore, risky to take the risk of staying away from fellowship.

Also, we should remember that what we receive in fellowship does not only depend on the speaker or teacher, but also the state of our life. "*Each person is individually responsible to God for having the proper attitude towards* His Word," said Florence L. Crawford, the founder of the Apostolic Faith work.

Carelessness in attending fellowship is another serious cause of spiritual dryness.

"For Christians, the church is a candle stick, a power source and somewhere to put down roots – so that you can stand, shine and grow." – Reinhard Bonnnke.

Conclusion:

In summary, Spiritual Dryness can directly, be the consequences of sin. And can, indirectly, be a degenerate of unknown carelessness. If prolonged, spiritual dryness can lead to spiritual death.

How Do I Know that I am Spiritually Dry?

(Symptoms of Spiritual Dryness)

"He livest long who liveth well: All else is being flung away; He liveth longest who can tell of true things truly done each day."
– Horatius Bonar

✓ *Why are you getting quite inconsistent in your personal fellowship with God?*

✓ *Why aren't you getting fresh revelations from the Word of God like before?*

✓ *Why is it becoming increasingly easy for you to do the things you wouldn't do as a Christian?*

✓ *Why has personal prayer and worship become so mechanical and boring?*

Chapter 24

Inconsistency in Personal Fellowship

Seek ye the LORD while he may be found, call ye upon him while he is near:

Isaiah 55:6

When spiritual dryness sets in, there is inconsistency in fellowship with God. In God's dealings with man, He loves more than many things, consistency in appointments.

And they heard the voice of the LORD God walking in the garden *in the cool of the day: Genesis 3:8a*

In the portion above, God was paying a visit to man in the Garden of Eden, as He had often done. The expression, **"in the cool of the day"** does not really imply a cool evening as one would quickly imagine, but has the import of, **"when the man was shut out of distractions."**

It means God had been coming down regularly to converse with man. He loves and honours man above all of His creation and so treats every appointment He has with man as very urgent and important.

Dr. Myles Munroe said, *"the opportunity for fellowship was part of the reason God created human beings."*

In fact, the Scripture declares that God so esteems man that He comes down to visit him every morning.

What is man, that thou shouldest magnify him? **And that thou shouldest visit him every morning....?** Job 7:17-18

When a Christian experiences spiritual dryness, there is broken fellowship between him and God.

In other words, there will be some days God will come for the visit without having good communication any longer. In most cases, He will come and find the man sleeping.

Imagine yourself having an appointment with a friend and at the agreed time, you are at his house, where the meeting was scheduled to take place, and find him sleeping comfortably. And not just that he is sleeping, but he is not even willing to get up to attend to you. That would not only be a disappointment but an embarrassment.

That is exactly what God faces daily when a man becomes spiritually dry.

In other instances, God visits, only to have the man talking with Him and sleeping at intervals, without imagining how He feels about it.

Pastor Richard Gazowsky related a very wonderful experience:

Once, while I was in Texas, I was invited to come and pray by a well-respected Pastor, who had a reputation for his prayer life. To my amazement, he fell asleep in the prayer room! Well, he called it "meditation" and I could emphasize with him, for I, also dozed off for a while. I just wonder what God thought about the whole thing.

I must quickly say here that, talking with God and sleeping in the process is not only an insult and embarrassment but also a big blow on His Personality.

The spiritually dry believer may actually try in most cases to continue in personal fellowship with God, but experiences a cut-and join relationship. Today he prays for one hour, tomorrow ten minutes. The day after tomorrow there's no quiet time and no prayer.

The next day, he has four minutes of prayer without Bible study. Another day, he just has a sort of short Bible reading and a short prayer. Some other day, he excuses himself with the fact that he slept very late the previous night, so there's nothing for God the next morning – no heavenly visit is welcome. This soon becomes a lifestyle.

The pastor who has these experiences prepares good and wonderful messages, and sleeps over them. He fails to understand that pastors who prepare good sermons and sleepover them all night long, often preach to men who appreciate good sermons and sleepover them all life long.

"...I aim at Thee, yet from thee stray." – Gerhard Tersteegen

The Deception of Sampson

The devil frequently deceives a spiritually dry Christian to believe that he is just as strong always. That is the same deception that was used on

Samson until he lost his eyes: his vision, focus, and Ministry.

And she said, The Philistines be upon thee, Samson. And he awoke out of his sleep, **and said, I will go out as at other times before, and shake myself.** *And he wist not that the LORD was departed from him.* **Judges 16:20**

At first, when a believer starts becoming inconsistent with God, there will surely be a witness of the spirit. Throughout the day he seems to feel like something is going wrong somewhere. He may feel some sorrow, guilt, or longing of some kind. In fact, he will appear to himself to be very incomplete in some way.

There is sometimes, such a serious stirring on the inside. If he is wise, he quickly responds to such bidding of the spirit and puts things in order concerning his spiritual life.

But most Christians become so busy they do not give the least response, and the bidding and stirring of the spirit decrease gradually until they are no more. After this negligence, the inconsistency becomes a part of their Christian lives and they tend to believe that all is going well, but no, it is not.

Beloved, never be deceived to believe that you can treat God like a dog: that you can desert Him when you feel like and call Him up again at any time. Or, that you can always break the appointments with Him and remake them at your convenience.

The fact that you can do a thing at some other time does not mean that it is the right time to do it. A time normally comes when you think God is there only to realize He is not.

I opened to my beloved; but my beloved had withdrawn himself, and was gone... I sought him, but I could not find him; I called him, but he gave me no answer. **Songs of Solomon 5:6**

Seek ye the LORD while he may be found, call ye upon him while he is near: **Isaiah 55:6**

Broken and inconsistent personal fellowship with God is a strong indication that you are spiritually dry.

"My spirit longs for Thee within my troubled breast, though I unworthy be of so Divine a Guest." – John Byron

An opportunity for God's visitation missed is an opportunity for Satan's devastation given.

Chapter 25

Lack of Fresh Understanding and Revelation from the Word

The entrance of they words giveth Light; it giveth understanding unto the simple.

– Psalms 119:130

Another familiar indication of spiritual dryness is the lack of fresh understanding of the Word of God.

You see, each time you sit down to study the Word of God, certain things take place. God releases the Spirit of wisdom and revelation to enlighten your understanding (Ephesians 1:17,

18). God has the power to open your understanding to understand His Word the way He wants you to.

Then opened he their understanding, *that they might understand the Scriptures. – Luke 24:25*

This is why you can read the same portion of Scripture at different times and have entirely different interpretations and revelations.

To be candid, every portion of Scripture will be interesting to you each time you read it because there is always something new you gain from it. What may seem like stories and formulated tales to someone else are shocking revelations on your part.

Of this, the Prophet Jeremiah wrote, *thy words were found, and I did eat them;*

and ***thy word was unto me the joy and rejoicing of mine heart...***" (Jer. 15:16).

In Lamentations 3:23 we read, "*They are new every morning*". God does not give us the same old love, mercy, or fire of yesterday. Each new day comes with a new experience.

In the same manner, He does not give us the same old revelations in the Word when we sit to study at His Feet.

Now, immediately spiritual dryness sets in, that fresh understanding of the Word is lost. You will notice that you seem to become so used to the Bible that most aspects of Scripture become uninteresting.

When you pick up the Bible, it just seems as if you know the entire New Testament and so, it is of no use spending your time on it. Any part of the New Testament you open to will appear to have been ready yesterday – the passage sounding so familiar.

When you open to the Old Testament, you notice there seem to be too many woes in Isaiah, too many judgments in Jeremiah, and too many Cherubim in Ezekiel. Nothing seems interesting.

The Bible then becomes like a storybook to you. The joy of reading and studying it is no longer there. You will even prefer to pick-up a Christian literature rather than read the Bible.

If you are a pastor, the Bible just becomes a reference book where you get messages to build others up while you languish in spiritual poverty.

Of course, no matter how much you can preach, that is something about you, that is not you. You can succeed in preaching and teaching and raising the hopes of people but they can never rise to the level of your preaching: they will only be like you and nothing more.

Water can only rise to its own level. The people you teach will only be like you and not like your message. The spiritual law cannot be broken – *"Like priest like people – Like pastor like congregation."*

A cat does not give birth to a young lion, but a cat; a monkey gives birth to a monkey, and so on. You can only reproduce your kind.

Teaching or preaching to innocent and perhaps ignorant souls from a dry spiritual life and hypocritical heart is like feeding a helpless man fainting from hunger with manna left overnight. A message given from a spiritually dry heart cannot nourish any life unto spiritual growth.

Who is blind as he that is perfect, *and blind as the LORD's servant? Seeing many things, but thou observest not;* ***opening the ears, but he heareth not.*** *Isaiah 42:19-20*

Now, many a time, a believer during his moments of freshness receives revelations in the Word of God even while the Minister is preaching on the pulpit. But the reverse is the case when he becomes spiritually dry.

When spiritually dry, he realizes that sometimes before the minister has given half the message he has slept and concluded two serious dreams, getting ready to get into the third adventure in the dream world only to be awakened by a 'praise the Lord' from a neighbor.

And immediately he awakes, he meets with a surprise: the same preacher on the same pulpit. The second immediate look he takes is at his wristwatch. Then one question quickly runs through his mind – "How long more is he still going on?"

He may not even remember the topic of the sermon, even when the topic has been given. It is as if the pastor is preaching the whole Bible, and the worst of it all is that the whole thing looks so familiar and uninteresting.

All of a sudden someone says 'let us rise up and pray,' or 'Bow your heads in prayer.' He bows his head or rises along with others, but begins to wonder what he is to pray for.

Beloved, immediately you realize that your love for personal as well as group Bible study is waxing cold, you should know that something is going wrong somewhere.

I opened my mouth, and panted: **for I longed for thy commandments. Psalms 119:131**

When this longing for the Word of God is lost, it is clear that dryness has set in.

"Where is the blessedness I knew when first I saw the Lord? Where is the Soul refreshing view Of Jesus and His Word?" – William Cowper

Beginning and ending the day with the Word is beginning and ending it with the Lord. Going through the day without the Word is going through it without the Lord; and one who has lost understanding of the Word has lost understanding of the Lord.

Chapter 26

Carnality

Because the carnal mind is enmity against God: for it is not subject to the law of God, neither indeed can be. So then they that are in the flesh cannot please God. **Romans 8:7-8**

Another good indication that you are becoming dry is the manifestation of the self-life. This can take place in many different ways of which I will consider but a few.

Complains and Excuses

The true Christian worker serves the Lord with such faithfulness as is not borne out of compulsion or propulsion by some external force or authority, but out of true and sincere love for God.

He is spiritually mature enough to know that faithfulness which has to do with man's compulsion or propulsion does not really spring out of true love in the heart and may have little or nothing to do with God.

He is least interested in the commendation that should come from any mortal as regards his responsibility in the vineyard. And so, he would do nothing to please any human, but his Master alone before whom he will someday stand to give an account, and also have his works tried.

He will, therefore, neither have the least time to complain about the slackness of others nor work to be seen or commended by any man. Prepared to serve the Lord despite the odds and hurts, he will rather prefer to be accused than give excuses why he failed in his responsibilities.

"Arm me with jealous care, as in thy sight to live; And O, thy servant, Lord, prepare, a strict account to give." – Charles Wesley

Once spiritually dry, the believer rather serves the Lord with much compulsion than his free will. And there is the likelihood of the average believer complaining of so many things, one of which may be his enormous spending on transportation to church.

You see friend, among other reasons God has given you money, is to save you some inconveniences, one of which may occasionally be paying your way to church. God may always miraculously open the doors of financial blessings just to help meet your need in that direction.

Once there's the feeling that too much is spent on transportation, for instance, and thus a 'curtailing system' should be introduced by missing come church activities, you may equally be shutting with your own hands, the doors that led to those Divine financial provisions.

Now, I am not saying that you should spend carelessly because you have to go to church, neither have I said that the whole money you have from your toils is for transportation to the church.

I have not also said that you should overwork yourself in the process of serving God. God does not want that. God rather demands that you freely and willingly offer yourself to serve Him. *"God does not force Himself upon you. He does not violate your will. He does not manipulate you,"* adds Dr. Wesley Duewel.

All I am presenting here is the fact that when spiritual dryness sets in, the little we do becomes so magnified in our imagination and over-exaggerated in our minds and understanding that we begin to murmur and complain about them.

Also, immediately you begin to give excuses why you are failing in your responsibilities, or why you cannot do what was handed into your hands, you must know that something is wrong with your spiritual life.

You must understand that whenever you are given a responsibility, God expects you to handle it in such a way that He can commend you even to generations yet unborn.

Of Moses, the Spirit testifies, "Moses *verily was faithful in all His house, as a servant...*" (Hebrews 3:5)

God is really not interested in our excuses. I am on the side of the Lady Apostle Helen Ukpabio when she says that, "*when we give excuses, we betray the confidence placed on us by God... At least God knew that those excuses were there before He picked us for the work...*"

And in the light of the judgment seat, Dr. W.E. Sangster says, "*How shall I feel at the judgment, if multitudes of missed opportunities pass before me in full review, and all my excuses prove to be disguises of my cowardice and pride?"*

The simple truth is this: Immediately we start making excuses and treasuring them, we must know that something has gone wrong with our spiritual lives.

"The devil works overtime to keep us griping and complaining, but God does not have any crying towels." – Ernest Gruen.

Testimonies

Another common manifestation of carnality is found in our testimonies.

Many times, in preparing to give a testimony, a believer so plans the way he will present his speech that he forgets important points and major events in his testimony.

Sometimes, in the process of doing this, he exaggerates on some points and thus paints them to help God look mightier than He actually is. In trying to tell men what God has done for him, he ends up telling them what He has not done for him.

But does God really need such help?

Will ye speak wickedly for God? and talk deceitfully for him? Job 13:7

Some Christians even tell outright lies in the name of testimonies.

*But ye are forgers of lies...***Job 13:4**

These are all but carnal manifestations.

If God has really done something for you and there is joy in your soul, you would not do any of these things. You will get all out to glorify God in every way.

You see, most Christians give testimonies without allowing others see what God has done for them. The whole testimony is filled with what they could do – so what did God do?

Every part of the testimony is packed with the words 'so I, as I, when I, then I, etc.,' It becomes a story of your personal strength and capability and not a testimony. This is clear evidence of self-manifestation.

And whatsoever ye do in word or deed, do it all to the glory of God - **Colossians 3:17**

Once your focus changes from how to satisfy God to how to satisfy yourself and other people, and make them feel comfortable with your preaching, singing, talking, walking, dancing, testimony etc., you should know that something is wrong somewhere.

"Ego, when it's untamed can become a monster." –Mathew Skariah

Men's Praises And Applause

Carnality can yet present itself in another way when spiritual dryness sets in, and that is when we begin to value the praise and applause of men than the commendation of God for our lives and Ministry.

When we begin to be more interested in what men think of us than in what God thinks. When we start putting in extra effort to impress men than God.

I think this is one of the greatest problems men of God are facing today: the desire for recognition and crave for fame.

*For they loved the praise of men more than the praise of God. – **John 12:43***

Let us take a practical example: a soloist leads in song for the choir, but it is just as if the people do not like the song. In fact, the faces of the people seem to be suggesting that the soloist is wasting their time and his too.

He concludes the song, with the atmosphere looking dull, and gets to his seat confused.

Later on, he gets on to interrogate some close friends about the ministration. The first person says, "*It* was very fine, only that the drummer was slower than you were."

He begins to blame the drummer.

The second person says, 'It was fine, but the keyboard was too loud.'

'Can't they ever control this keyboard volume?" the soloist laments.

The third person says, 'everything, including the instruments was okay, it was just the way you kept your right leg when you were taking the second solo.'

Again he screams, "Oh, no wonder that man in the front row was looking at me like that!"

But, for God's sake, why all these interrogations? If he has prayed and ministered his song, does he need the approval and applause of a man as a confirmation of what God has done?

A.W. Tozer has said that, "*the man who is elated by success and cast down by failure is still a carnal man.*"

And Thomas Kempis adds that, "*He who minds neither praise nor blame possesses great peace of heart.*"

These are true.

God works in any way He chooses to. His move can be a silent seed sown in somebody's heart somewhere and can also be a violent and radical manifestation. But, you do not need to be bothered about that. All you need is to do what He has asked you to do. Working for God by men's reactions is not only carnal but also a slight on His power.

You need to understand that, "*the race is neither to the swift nor the battle to the strong. It is not of him that wills, not of him that runs, but of God that shows mercy.*"

If men do not appreciate you, what tells you that God does not?

If men do not clap for you, do angels not also clap?

These feelings are but carnal manifestations. And in fact, you never know how great the Lord is making you until you keep the eyes of your mind off the praises of men.

Frederick William Faber, the songwriter wrote:

"Then learn to scorn the praise of men, and learn to lose with God; for Jesus won the world through shame, and beckons thee His road."

"Praise adds nothing to your holiness, nor does blame take

anything from it." – Thomas A Kempis

Chapter 27

Prayer Becomes Mechanical

O God, thou art my God; early will I seek thee: my soul thirsteth for thee, my flesh longeth for thee in a dry and thirsty land, where no water is; **Psalms 63:1**

Mechanical prayer is one of the 'easiest-to-detect' symptoms of spiritual dryness.

When is Prayer Mechanical?

Prayer is mechanical when it lacks unction, faith, power, and brokenness. When it lacks the propelling Spirit – the sweet Spirit of God that leads the human spirit into the 'God realm'. Thus, it becomes like a forced vibration, so that one merely forces himself into it even when he knows that he really does not have any willingness in the least to do so.

In most cases too, one may really have the willingness and deep desire to pray, but soon realizes a few minutes after starting that it suddenly becomes so uninteresting. And the more he tries to push ahead, the more evident the emptiness felt within becomes.

Now, I will use three simple ways to give a clearer view of when prayer is mechanical.

When Worship Seems Boring

The Christian who is in tune with the Spirit of God often notices that he awakes from sleep most mornings with a worship song, a hymn, or praise in his innermost being. With such a song in his innermost being comes a deep desire to get enveloped in the glory of God's Divine presence.

Carried away by such an intense desire, he discovers that everything else seems so secondary. He realizes he feels like nothing else but praising and worshipping and telling his Lord how much he loves Him, from the depth of his soul.

In many instances he would want to get into praying, only to realize that he ends up worshipping Him more and more as his love for Him intensifies.

Hence, the more he sings from his heart of hearts, the more he feels like doing so.

By the time he finally gets into praying, he just gets along because he is already enveloped by the Divine presence. So, he finds such great joy and confidence as he presents one request after the other, before the throne of grace.

And, he finds much more joy, when the Holy Ghost quickens different requests into his spirit man, asking him to pray or intercede for someone or something else.

Prayer becomes mechanical when worship seems boring. It is not as though the desire to worship is altogether lost – far from it! You would always want to worship, but the emptiness you feel as you take one song after the other is what really sends the feeling that it is a waste of time.

You can really try to persevere, and take a few worship songs along with much yawning and then burst into some kind of forceful praying. So, at one time you may try to pray as fast as a sewing machine and at some other time as forceful as a weight lifter, in a bit to improve the condition, only to realize how tiring and hypocritical it becomes.

You are most often left to wonder at the end, why the clock could only prove you to have prayed for only five to ten minutes, when you felt you must have exhausted some good forty-five minutes or an hour after such a terrible struggle.

That prayer is mechanical.

"What peaceful hours I once enjoyed! How sweet their memory still! But they have left an aching void The world can never fill." – William Cowper

Lack of Brokenness

It is brokenness in God's presence that allows you to enjoy fellowship in His presence. It is your brokenness that attracts God's attention to forgive and to give.

*The sacrifices of God are **a broken spirit: a broken and a contrite heart**, O God, thou wilt not despise.* ***Psalms 51:17***

Prayer is mechanical when it is done without brokenness. And you aren't broken in prayer when you pray with your lips while your heart is far away from what you say.

Listen! The broken Christian has his mouth and heart in perfect agreement and unity. He says with his mouth only that which he utters from his heart.

A believer is truly broken in God's presence when these two parts of him – the mouth and the heart – are in agreement, the one with the other. When they are in agreement, they carry his emotions, feelings, and intellect along.

The result is that every word that comes out of his mouth is sincerely meant in the heart. The expressions of his lips are just the true confessions of his heart before the Lord.

Henry Wadsworth Longfellow long understood much of this truth when he wrote, "*You know, I say just what I think and nothing less. And when I pray, my heart is in my prayer. I cannot say one thing and mean another.*"

The unbroken Christian approaches the Divine Presence with nothing other than sense knowledge. He speaks with his Master with such words as lack the true, deep, and sincere affection. And he often thinks that the greater the volume of his words, the more valuable his prayer.

Really, God would have no time with the sacrifice of fools, that is, speaking with the mouth such large volumes of words, which are neither rooted in the spirit nor meant in the heart.

Sometimes, you find yourself praying in one location while in your thoughts you visit relations in another city.

Or, maybe you're praying in your bedroom but in your thoughts, you're withdrawing money from the bank.

The pastor prays in his closet while in thought, he settles serious disputes between some stubborn members of his congregation.

These are no more than the fool's sacrifice, of which God would rather not have a part.

In the spiritual sense of it, if the heart carries no burden, the mouth can express no burden, because it is only out of the abundance of the heart that the mouth speaks. Where the heart has nothing that can move God, the mouth will have nothing that can move God. We do not draw water from an empty well - do we? Of course not!

Sister Choi - the mother of Dr. Paul Yonggi Cho - was not wrong, when with such unflinching certainty she said, *"If it does not come from the heart, God does not listen."*

The heart of the wise teacheth his mouth, and addeth learning to his lips. - **Proverbs 16:23**

Lack of Inward Confidence

When prayer is not mechanical, there is an inward joy and conviction after each request is presented before the Lord.

The joy of forgiveness is equally experienced after a sober confession of sin along with true repentance.

There is that faith beyond any reasonable doubt, after each request is presented, that God has heard, and not only heard but has answered; and has not only answered but has answered either, *"Yes, I'll do it, or yes, I have done it!"*

By the end of such praying, there is the feeling of a heavy burden being lifted off. One feels happier, lighter, and filled with assurance all through.

The contrary is the case when prayer is mechanical. Fear replaces faith and doubt replaces confidence in God. With such a lack of confidence, even in the immediate cleansing power of the Blood, the guilt of a sin already confessed and repented of, is allowed to persist and loom the spirit, so much that the same sin is confessed almost every time the throne of grace is approached.

Conclusion:

Watch your life very carefully. Do you have some or all of these experiences? How has your relationship with God in prayer been, recently?

"Really understanding our problem is a long way on the road toward solving it." –Mathew Skariah

If SPIRITUAL DRYNESS has crept into your life unnoticed, you must deal with it and straighten your relationship with God.

Please pray this simple prayer with me:

Lord, I thank You for showing me my true state today. Help me, Dear Lord, to find my way back to a deeper and more loving relationship with You, in Jesus' Name. Amen!

How to Overcome and Recover from Spiritual Dryness

✔ When personal needs and demands overtake the Ministerial mind; when Christians measure success by worldly standards; when decisions for spiritual things are looked at, judged, and considered by sight and not by faith; then of a truth, **a state of DRYNESS has set in**.

✔ **When God is only given a second and not a first place**, then, one must accept the truth and quickly seek for restoration and refreshing.

Chapter 28

Overcoming Spiritual Dryness

Overcoming Spiritual Dryness is simple. A careful study of the causes of dryness and handling them does the miracle. If you can understand what leads to spiritual dryness, as enumerated in the second volume of this series, and avoid them like a plague, you can live a fruitful life.

For instance, if you understand that fasting makes your spirit sharper and more sensitive to the Spirit of God, you can overcome dryness in your prayer life by setting aside special seasons of prayer and fasting.

If fasting can help to maintain spiritual freshness, it stands to reason that the lack of consistent consecration fasts can cause dullness or dryness in your prayer life.

This is just a simple example. And I have given this example to help you look back into the causes of dryness and ask yourself what you can do to avoid getting in that rut.

Some time ago, a young lady came over to see me after reading the first edition of Overcoming Spiritual Dryness. She was obviously so broken and needed help. But after listening to her, I realized that, in the first instance, she shouldn't have been in the place she found herself at all.

She narrated the experience of always travelling with her boss, who was also a

Christian in the same assembly where she worshipped. Every time they travelled, the boss would always get over and start touching her here and there.

According to her, she kept on resisting him, until the day came when they travelled somewhere and when he came touching her, she gave in to him.

Thereafter she felt such crushing guilt that left her spiritually devastated. Her prayer life and everything declined so badly that she could feel her distance from God.

Now, I said at the beginning that she didn't need to get in that place at all; yes, because she could already read the handwriting on the wall.

I know she was in a job, but the moment she realized the consistent advances of her boss, she either needed to stop travelling with him or opt for another job. Nothing is worth your relationship with God – NOTHING!

Rather than do that, she continued to endure her boss' advances. And the more she endured it, the weaker her resistance became, until she gave in to the compromise. Though she allowed it once, the devastating consequences on her spiritual life lasted a long time.

We have to understand that sin builds momentum with each compromise. It's like a web of events. Every time you allow it, more loops are added to the web. It keeps building up until it forms what the Apostle Paul would describe as "an entanglement."

This young lady's narration shows us it's best to get rid of something that pushes us into a position of guilt and pain than wait to repent from it. The best way to overcome spiritual dryness is to never allow anything that could cause it.

That said, I'll advise that you take out time and check whatever in your life easily leads to the place of dryness, and deal decisively with it.

In this brief volume, I'll spend a bit of time talking about recovering from Spiritual Dryness. Let's meet over in the next chapter.

Chapter 29

Recovering from Spiritual Dryness

Just after being cured of a sickness, a person begins to recover from it and again regain his health, which must have gone down in the course of the sickness.

Equally too, as you recover from spiritual dryness you begin to enjoy wonderful experiences. In this chapter I discuss two important experiences among the many you will have during your recovery.

The Spirit's Refreshing

And He shall come unto us as the rain, as the latter and former rain unto the earth. – **Hosea 6:3b**

As you recover from spiritual dryness, there is sure going to be the joy of being forgiven right within your soul.

Bless the Lord, O my soul and forget not all his benefits: who forgiveth all thine iniquities; who healeth all thy diseases – **Psalms 103:2,3**

There will be a new and fresh desire for the presence of the Lord and the Word of God. You will enjoy deep fellowship with the Lord as well as with the brethren.

There will be a new, greater and deeper love for the Lord.

A new passion for souls will crop up within you.

All these things will come because there has been a fresh shower upon your spirit by God's Spirit.

Once the rain of the Spirit falls on you, there is an instant transfer from spiritual dryness to spiritual freshness.

Have you ever seen a grass field burnt by fire? How does that same grass field look after some time when rain falls upon it?

The grasses begin to come up again, and very fresh looking this time around. Although it may not take place in one day, it is certain that they will gradually grow back into a fresh-looking and beautiful lawn.

Until the spirit be poured upon us from on high, and the wilderness be a fruitful field, and the fruitful field be counted for a forest. **Isaiah 32:15**

Remember that spiritual dryness isn't spiritual death. Though you were spiritually dry, you were not spiritually dead.

You were dry but your roots were still trying to survive the unfavourable condition by adaption. They still had some water and nutrients from the soil to live and depend on.

You were still going to Church, and fortunately attending some services; that was why you were still able to pray a little, read the Bible, and so on. Your roots still had some water to live on.

Your returning to the Lord brings the rain. What the rain does is revive your roots, and quicken them to produce sprouts, which then shoot into green vegetation.

These may not all take place in one day but will progressively and certainly come to pass, and once more your spirit will bathe in an atmosphere of spiritual freshness.

He hasn't lost His touch; I've never felt love so much. Just like the year's first rain, Refreshing my life again... - ***Vincent Chiori***

Only a man that has experienced the wilderness understands what it means to have the rain again.

You Will Be Built-Up

If you will return unto the almighty you will be built up. **–Job 22:23**

When you return to the Lord, He will build you up again: He will build your prayer life again; He will build you up in His Word again, and in many aspects of your Christian life.

Just like the growth process, the building process does not take place all at once, but gradually.

The question is, how long does it take?

Well, that will depend on two factors. How long it takes a person recovering from a certain sickness to build up again in health depends, to a great extent, on how long the person has been ill, and the availability of the essential things needed to build him\her up again.

If two people were suffering from the same ailment, one for two months, and the other for a week, you would expect the latter to get built up in health faster than the former – assuming they both recovered at the same time.

Let us also assume that they both suffered this ailment for an equal number of months – say two - and one person feeds on some balanced diet and fruits daily, while the other feeds on carbohydrate thrice daily.

You would expect the first person to recover and get healthy within a short time, right?

These two factors also strongly determine how long it will take you to get built up again. You must understand that God does not determine how long it will take you to get built up, but you.

Try to understand how long you have been spiritually dry.

Begin to get serious in fellowship, attend prayer meetings, diligently study the Word, organize personal retreats, get many tapes (messages) listen and pray with them.

Get some Christian literature that can build your spiritual life and read them. Have a specific time to fast and pray personally and learn to spend more time with the Lord.

These things and many others will help accelerate your getting built up.

And the Gentiles shall come to thy light, and kings to the BRIGHTNESS OF THY RISING. – **Isaiah 60:3**

To every failing then, there is a rising. For every wilderness experience is a

Canaan ahead. With every discovery comes a recovery, and the once overcome can be the overcomer.

A true and effective 'building' by God is always the result of a true and effective 'yielding' to God; for God only completely builds a man who completely yields to Him.

Chapter 30

Basking in a New Glory

Arise and Shine; for your light has come and the glory of the Lord has risen upon you. **Isaiah 60:1**

Many a time, God allows us to pass through certain things so that He might prune or cut us to size again.

Spiritual dryness is actually dangerous and terrible too. But God sometimes does allow us to pass through some of these things so that He might humble us, show how over-self-confident, careless and spiritually myopic we have become, or let us know that we are drifting away from our roots.

Sometimes, it allows us to be much more careful.

I do believe that some of the things we pass through are actually preparatory grounds for a higher level of service or relationship with God.

I do not, however, imply that God only uses bitter spiritual experiences, trials and difficulties to lift us to higher heights or lead us into a deeper relationship or closer walk with Him. But when He does, "*we must*" as Watchman Nee once said, "*realize that all the experiences, difficulties and trials from the Lord are for our highest good.*"

I do think that most of the times that God allows us to pass through spiritual dryness, He is simply telling us that the time is ripe for us to take another step unto a new and higher level of walk with Him.

I feel God does this because some of us get too quickly satisfied with the level we find ourselves in our relationship with Him, with so little or no desire for something greater.

I quite agree with the words of Dr. Wesley Duewel: *"We are too easily satisfied and glory in occasional past moments when God touched us by His power. We have become too complacent and too easily satisfied with minimum manifestations of His power."* And this 'complacency' A. W. Tozer says, *"Is a deadly foe of all spiritual growth."*

It is not God's will that we dwell for so long on a particular level of spiritual experience or relationship with Him, but rather, that we grow and experience higher heights and grounds as there is always a higher ground.

It was Dennis Kinlaw who very assuredly said, *"He does not want me to be the same next week that I was last week."* This is the simple truth!

Nevertheless, when we heartily return to the Lord after a bitter experience of spiritual dryness, He does not put us again on the former level we were. He does not take us back to where we were before that painful experience; rather, He takes us to a new level entirely.

We do not relate with Him anymore in prayer the same way that we knew to do but deeper and much more loving than we ever could do.

We develop a deeper longing for the Word, deeper than we have ever had.

Deeper revelations start flooding our inner man, and certain verses of Scripture we had once known become almost entirely new because of the depth of revelations we become exposed to.

In fact, everything about our relationship with Him assumes a new dimension.

He clothes us with a new glory. He does not give again the former glory, but a new glory – a latter glory. And He had already promised us that the latter glory shall be greater than the former.

The latter glory of this house shall be greater than the former, says the Lord of hosts; - **Haggai 2:9a** (Berkeley)

Now friend, you do not have to be ignorant; there is a new glory overshadowing you. You are already basking in it. Do not allow the devil and his chief messenger, guilt, to rob or cheat you. The road to the realm of higher relationship and a closer walk with God is already littered with so many carcasses of sincere believers who gave up because they listened to the devil and yielded to guilt.

Have nothing to do with whatever the devil has to say. Tell him, *"Devil, I listened to you when I was down there, but now I am up here! You are not any longer my match, neither will you ever be, so GET LOST!"*

Listen! the devil has nothing to say other than to talk about the past. But you are no longer in the past. The past is past and your past is as past as "the past" itself.

The ever-growing spiritual life is a fast-moving vehicle loaded with new and magnificent visions for tomorrow with no vacancy for the past.

The ministry continues. Greater challenges and exploits lie ahead. No matter how odd the wilderness experiences have been, they were just for the wilderness, the journey to Canaan continues.

Canaan is still to be possessed. Stop wasting your time worrying about the past! "*Your time is too valuable to waste worrying about how dumb you were to do what you did,*" Bill Wayman adds.

Refuse to believe how bad you think about yourself and begin to believe how good God thinks about you.

Refuse to believe what the devil says you are and believe who God says you are.

It is true that you fumbled with the ball, but you have picked it up again running. As you run with it, your interest is not in how you fumbled with it or who made you fumble. Your interest is the goal post. YES!

Refuse to see the weak and fallen you of yesterday and see the strong and risen you of today. In Jeremiah 8:4 we read, *Thus saith the Lord;* "*shall they fall and not arise?*"

Refuse to act like the guilt, fearful, sad-feeling and depressed you of yesterday and act like the forgiven, bold, and joy-bubbling you of today.

Refuse to accept the disdaining philosophies of men about your past, present and future, and accept the Word of God for your life.

Don't waste your time crying over spilt milk. Get back into the race ad give it all you've got.

But the LORD says, "Do not cling to events of the past or dwell on what happened long ago. Watch for the new thing I am going to do. It is happening already – you can see it now!" **–Isaiah 43:18-19** (Goodnews)

A greater glory is come upon you. You are not the same "you" of yesterday. The "you" of yesterday was of yesterday, but a new "you" is here today – better know this.

Do not confess again like the "you" of yesterday. Change your confession.

Do not say any longer, "*I am fallen,*" but say, "I am arisen to shine again!"

Do not say, "*The devil has gotten me,*" but say like David, "*laugh not at me my enemy, for though seven times I fall, I shall yet arise!*"

Do not say, "*I feel so weak I can't pray,*" but say, "*I feel so strong I can pray all night!*"

If at anytime the desire for the old sinful habit tries to crop up within you, neither be afraid nor lament over it, but be bold to say, "*I am too holy for that, devil! I am a fearful weapon in the hands of a holy God.*"

See yourself in the greater glory!

His glory is risen and shall remain upon you as long as you abide in His grace, for on your own you can do nothing.

The closer you get, the more you will see His Glory, the Glory of the Only Begotten of the Father; the Glory of the soon coming King!

No matter how many times a man has fallen, he is not termed 'defeated' by the kingdom of darkness until he refuses to rise again. For it is not the man that falls down that is defeated, but the man that stays down after falling. The Spirit says "Arise!"

Congratulations!

Beloved, I congratulate you for finding time to go through this book, and I believe your life will never remain the same.

If this book has blessed or helped you in any way, I'll GREATLY APPRECIATE if you can share your testimony by writing an honest review OR leave a simple feedback on amazon.com in order to help more people discover this book and experience a transformation in their life, too. I'll also personally read your review. *Thank you.*

<u>THIS IS VERY IMPORTANT!</u>

Beloved, you need to surrender your life to the Lordship of Jesus Christ by accepting His sacrificial death on Calvary for you or you need to re-dedicate your life to Jesus Christ.

Pray this prayer with me:

Lord Jesus, I come before You today to surrender my life completely to you. I have lived a self-centred life that is far separated from God, I have had priorities that are not eternity-centred, I have always lived in rebellion, disobedience and sin up till now.

Lord, I am sorry for the way that I have lived and I ask for your forgiveness and mercy. Lord, please cleanse my sins by your blood and take your place of leadership and rulership in my life.

Fill my heart Lord with the right desires and priorities. Deliver me from the vanity and fantasies of this world.

Give me the grace to say no to sin and compromise. Give me the grace to live in righteousness and represent you well in my world.

Help me to escape the tragedy of eternity in hell. Help me Lord to make heaven at the end of my journey on earth.

Help me Lord to live both in consciousness of your presence and of eternity.

Continuously reveal to me everything that would make me unworthy of Heaven.

Thank you Lord for hearing and answering me in Jesus' Name I pray, Amen.

If you have prayed this payer, please do the following:

1. Send us your name, phone number, and contact address by email: id_degt@yahoo.com or by phone: +995 568 286 737.

2. Become serious with God by identifying with a righteousness and eternity-conscious church.

3. Study your Bible daily to receive a word from God.

4. Speak to God daily in prayer and let Him know your feelings and challenges.

5. Disconnect from every wrong association. Don't follow them to hell if they won't follow you to Heaven.

6. Speak to others about God. Share your testimony of transformed life. Be

instrumental in assisting someone to escape hell.

7. Repent promptly. Do not sleep over unconfessed sins. Apply the blood over your soul for cleansing continuously. Live eternity ready.

The Lord bless you.

ABOUT THE AUTHOR

Idongesit Okpombor is a Christian, a well sought-after speaker in Christian conferences, a life coach, author, husband, father, and the CEO, Kings View Publishing House; an award-winning, high-ranking, Global Publishing Firm established in 2007.

Idongesit is the author of the bestsellers, ***<u>DARE TO BE DIFFERENT!</u>****,* ***<u>SEVEN WAYS TO MAKE YOUR YEAR COUNT</u>****,* ***<u>MAKING YOUR YEAR PROSPEROUS</u>****, and more.*

He is married to Sheelah, an educationist and also an avid writer. They are blessed with three versatile children.

Connect with the author at:

id_degt@yahoo.com